AQA GCSE ENGLISH LANGUAGE STUDY AND REVISION GUIDE

Get inside the examiner's head and raise your grade!

DARREN COXON

For Julija, who always makes me watch my language.

Copyright © 2018 Darren Coxon
All rights reserved.
ISBN: 9781724132611

🌸 Created with Vellum

WHY YOU'RE READING THIS

Well, here we are.

I'm guessing you're reading this because you're stressing out about your rapidly approaching English Language exam.

Or maybe you're a teacher stressing out about your students' rapidly approaching English Language exam.

Or maybe you're a parent stressing out about the fact your kid's not stressing out about…

Anyway, it's likely there's some stress around.

Well, stress no more. As this little guide will ease your mind and make you smile again. You see, I've been doing this for years. About twenty to be precise.

I'm not in the classroom any more (I manage schools in the UK and across the world) but in my career as an English teacher I reckon I've put something in the region of a thousand kids through this exam.

Over that time I worked out what is inside that strange place we know of as 'the examiner's head' so know what students need to know to get a decent grade.

Maybe not always the top grade, but a decent one nonetheless. And I'm guessing that for many of you reading this guide that would be enough.

WHAT THIS GUIDE IS ABOUT

This isn't like a normal revision guide. You may have already worked that one out. I'm not setting out to teach you the entire syllabus. That was your teacher's job.

What I'd like to do is give you some tips for how to think like an examiner: how to write so that every single sentence gets you a mark. Because otherwise it's a waste of ink on paper.

The main problem with English Language lessons is that they can often be quite dull. I know, I taught enough of them. Not all: I had some brilliant lessons where we debated interesting topics and my students wrote some amazing persuasive arguments.

But a lot of them are a slog: as much for the teachers as the students. Most English teachers are literature graduates - we love books, not necessarily grammar.

This is a shame, as the skills you learn in this course are important. Take the ones this exam tests you on - I use them every day:

- Being able to read something quickly and summarise the main points;

- Picking out bits of a text then exploring them in my own words;
- Structuring my writing for the intended audience and to maximise impact;
- Writing clearly and coherently;
- Writing about some people on a bus (ok maybe not this one).

So, it does make sense to ensure you have these skills. Trust me.

If there is one piece of wisdom I can pass on to you, it is this: to be successful in life, you have to know the rules of the game. You have (in the words of Rage Against the Machine) to 'know your enemy'.

You have to work out what the examiner wants. So, come with me while we enter their mysterious world. Who knows, you might learn something that makes a genuine difference to your grade. I hope so.

OVERVIEW

OVERVIEW OF THE EXAM

Before we get stuck in, here's a quick overview of the two papers. It's worth spending a few moments looking at how they differ, so that we approach them in the correct way to maximise our success.

Both Papers are divided into two sections: A and B. And each Paper is worth 80 Marks - again, divided into two: 40 marks for Section A and 40 marks for Section B. Here they are in more detail:

PAPER 1: 'EXPLORATIONS IN CREATIVE READING AND WRITING'

Section A - Reading

You have 4 questions to answer:

1. Picking out information
2. Explaining how language is used for effect - how the words work
3. Explaining how structure is used for effect - how the words are put together
4. Agreeing or disagreeing with a statement using evidence from the text

Section B - Creative Writing

You'll have a choice of two questions: one will be based on a photo, and one will be based on a stimulus question. They'll both link in some way to the subject of Section A. Both will probably be quite boring. But more on that later.

PAPER 2: 'WRITER'S VIEWPOINTS AND PERSPECTIVES'

Section A - Reading

And again, 4 questions (you can't fault them for consistency). The two texts/sources will be on the same topic but will differ in period - usually one from the 19th Century and one from the 20th or 21st Century:

1. Choosing true statements about one of the sources
2. Summarising two sources: different perspectives on the same subject
3. Analysing one section of one of the sources in more detail
4. Comparing how the two sources deal with the same subject

Section B - Writing

You'll probably have no choice: it will be a piece of non-fiction writing that takes the theme of Section A. It might be more interesting than Paper 1. It might not.

In a nutshell, Paper 1 will focus on fiction, and Paper 2 on non-fiction. Both are testing you on how well you read, then how well you write.

The problem I always had with the kids I taught was that they often didn't see the point in revising for this exam. Particularly if they were good at literature, they thought they could just wing it and then focus their attention on revising for literature.

And guess what? They usually bombed their mock. And then they revised.

Because this exam is all about **technique**. About how to ensure everything you write ticks a box. We'll talk a lot more about that as we go on.

Now let's look at everyone's favourite subject. Assessment Objectives. No, really. They are interesting.

AO, AO, IT'S OFF TO WORK WE GO

Yes, I know. When your teacher mentioned Assessment Objectives you probably disappeared into your head and didn't come out again until break. And I don't blame you. This is a shame: they are quite important, as they give us a clear insight into the examiner's head.

Unsurprisingly, assessment objectives (AOs) are the objectives you're assessed on. In other words, you learn stuff and the exam tests to see whether you know it.

And as there are hundreds of thousands of poor souls like you who are going through these exams, and hundreds of teachers paid peanuts to mark them, there has to be consistency.

Let's take a moment to meet a generic exam marker.

MEET JEFF

Jeff is an English teacher. He's been in the job four years, still enjoys it, and is ready to take his career to the next level. His head of department tells him that in order to really understand the syllabus he teaches he should become an exam marker.

Jeff agrees and attends a course which teaches him how to accurately mark exam papers.

The holidays roll around and a large box arrives at Jeff's home. In it are exam papers from students he does not know. Hundreds of them. Along with the papers are mark schemes and other admin needed for him to accurately mark.

He begins to wonder whether he made a mistake.

Now imagine this. Jeff is at home while his family are at the beach and his mates at the pub (cliches, but go with me here). He has to go through these hundreds of papers and apply the same set of criteria to each.

So it is vitally important that he has a standard formula to work through. And this formula begins with assessment objectives.

This is so that, when Jeff marks a paper, he does it in the exact same way as Jane (she's another examiner - keep up) and John (ditto).

That's what AOs are. Yes, they're there to show the world that you have all these skills, but to Jeff, Jane and John they're a tick list.

As honestly, they don't care whether you actually have these skills - they don't know you so why should they? They just want to tick the AOs off and get onto paper number 287. Just 223 to go….

If you start thinking like this from the start, you realise that AOs can be your friends. Because if everything you write ticks one of those bad boys, you're home and dry. I mean it. **Do not write a single sentence unless it gets you a mark.**

I'm not going to go through them all one by one and explain them here, as you need to see them in action.

What I will do is refer to them so you can see that, by following the tips and tricks I outline in the coming pages, you can't help but tick all those boxes and get the grade you so richly deserve.

8 HACKS FOR YOUR ENGLISH EXAM

Before we get under the bonnet and check out all those dirty, oily questions to see how we might answer them brilliantly, let's look at the paintwork and see how comfy the seats are (I think I've stretched that metaphor far enough).

Even if you give up after reading this section, the following eight hacks should help you a lot.

#1 MAKE SURE YOU READ THE FRONT PAGE OF THE EXAM PAPER

Read the front page. Carefully. Then read it again. Why? Because it's important, that's why. Here's a set, with an examiner's thoughts in brackets:

- Answer all questions (*as otherwise what was the point of us writing them*)
- Use black ink (*not sparkly purple ink that smells of artificial blueberries as it makes my house smell horrible and gives me a rash*)
- Don't write outside the box (*as we examiners never colour outside the lines*)

- Don't use tippex - cross out (*tippex is evil and pointless and sticks pages together*)
- Look at how you're being assessed - reading in section A, writing in section B (*just so that I am actually able to mark your answer and not hunt around for ways to give you marks*)

And the best reason for reading it through? Bullet pointed lists have been scientifically proven to calm you down (probably). I know you feel calmer after reading the above. Don't deny it.

#2 UNDERSTAND EXACTLY HOW MANY MINUTES YOU SHOULD SPEND PER MARK

Look at the number of marks per question, and give yourself about one minute per mark (this works for AQA but may differ for other exam boards). You have one hour 45 minutes for each paper. You're expected to spend about 45 minutes on each section with 15 minutes for reading. There are 40 marks per Section. So don't spend 20 minutes on question 1 when it's only worth 4 marks.

That would be a bit like paying £20 for a packet of crisps.

#3 MAXIMISE YOUR EFFECTIVENESS IN READING THE PASSAGE IN PAPER 1

A controversial tip for you - don't read the extract before you start to work through the questions. Whaaat? Why? That makes no sense!

Well, it does actually. As you've no idea what you're looking for until you read through the questions carefully. And you'll have exam nerves which makes everything a bit foggy. So if you read through the passage cold it just won't go in. And probably stress you out even more.

So - go straight to question 1. And only read the number of lines it tells you to read. Now, underline the words and phrases that answer the question. And then write those in the space on the answer paper. Four marks. Bosh.

Now on to question 2. Same again. Question 3? If it asks you to read the whole thing then do so. And because you've carefully read the first two sections you should feel like you know it pretty well.

Remember: play the game. Maximise your time.

#4 UNDERSTAND EXACTLY WHAT EACH QUESTION IS ASKING YOU TO DO

Make sure you understand the differences between each question. This is important. For example, in Paper 1:

- Question 1 asks you to find some words and phrases and list them
- Question 2 asks you to analyse (explain) how the writer creates certain effects. This is different from question 1 - it wants you to explain in your own words how certain words and phrases create a certain impression on the reader.
- Question 3 asks you to talk about structure.
- Question 4 gives you a statement and asks you to agree or disagree with it.

I'll give you some worked through examples later which should help.

#5 WATCH YOUR LANGUAGE

I don't mean avoid swearing in the exam room. You can't anyway, as you're not allowed to speak (unless it's that voice in your head in which case that one can swear as much as it likes). I mean make sure you use language-y language.

What do I mean? Well, rather than saying things like 'the *word* 'rough' suggests that.....', say 'the *adjective* 'rough'...'

Try where possible to name parts of each sentence. Talk about adjectival clauses and complex sentences. Mention simile, metaphor and alliteration.

Whether it's prose, poetry or drama, using these words will bring you riches. Or at least marks.

#6 KNOW THE DIFFERENCE BETWEEN SECTION A AND SECTION B

This one seems obvious, but again it's important. Section A tests you on your reading. Section B on your writing. Any spelling, punctuation and grammar mistakes you make in Section A won't be so important - it's the quality of your reading and ideas that count.

Section B? Spelling, punctuation, grammar, layout, clear handwriting: worth almost half the marks. 16 out of 40 to be precise.

Write well in Section B.

#7 BORING IN DOESN'T HAVE TO MEAN BORING OUT

Let's be honest. The Paper 1 Section B writing prompts given to 'stimulate' your imagination are often dull. I mean, even Stephen King would struggle to come up with something sparkling and original when asked to write about the weather. Or a train. Or a train in some weather.

But guess what? Stephen King isn't in this exam (would be weird if he was, wouldn't it? Might be creepy). You are.

So it's up to you to impress the examiner with something compelling and entertaining. Not throw up your arms and shout 'the muse cannot visit me in these conditions'.

Remember our friends Jeff and Jane? 500 exam papers. 500 descriptions of a train in some weather.

Let yours be the one that jumps out and makes Jeff spill his flat white on his chinos (blatant teacher stereotype).

Let yours be so full of originality that he laughs and claps his hands together and shouts 'finally, here it is!'

At least let yours be the one he can actually read.

Think about ways you can make the opening sentences interesting. Maybe a one word sentence. Or start halfway through something happening. Or half way through a conversation.

More on this later.

#8 GIVE YOURSELF TIME AT THE END OF THE EXAM TO READ THROUGH

I know what you're thinking. He cannot be serious. No student in the history of students has ever actually done this in the exam. Have they? Allow 5 minutes to read through your exam. Ha!

But look at it like this: if you were only to read through Section B, realised that you'd forgotten to put in paragraphs, then used the universal // symbol between sentences that means 'oops I should have put a paragraph in here', you could raise your grade from a maximum 5 (C) to a 7 or 8.

I'm serious. This is the land of examiners we're talking about. It's not like the real world.

PAPER 1, SECTION A

PAPER 1: A QUICK INTRO

I hope those 8 hacks were helpful. Now to an actual example of how to put some of this into practice.

Now that we are a few years into the new specification, we have more resources available to us. In the last edition of this guide, I used AQA's specimen exam papers. This time I'll be using the June 2017 papers.

No doubt you're familiar with these already, but I hope the approaches I outline will enable you to nail the exam you'll sit. The nice thing about language is it's quite formulaic, and every year the exams will be broadly the same.

What I want to do is show you how to approach each question from beginning to end, so that when the examiner comes to mark your paper their pen flies over the paper dropping marks onto it like fairy dust. If exam markers were fairies. Which I don't technically think they can be.

One more thing before we dive under the exam bonnet. My approach might be different from how your teacher has taught you to approach this exam.

And you might read my ideas and think 'nope, that's not for me'. And that's fine. I won't take offence.

But: I can pretty well guarantee there'll be something in here that will help. So, have an open mind while you read, and imagine how they might be of use when you're sitting at that stupidly small, wobbly exam desk with someone sniffing a few rows back from you (yes, we invigilators dislike these people as much as you do: please take tissues into your exam).

Remember - you are trying to get inside a dark and lonely world: the world of the examiner's head. So put aside all emotion, take a deep breath, and let's play the examiner game!

SECTION A

As we know (and if we don't then where have we been since page one), Section A is the reading section. What does this mean? Of course, you're not just going to read. You're going to show you understand what you've read.

And how will you do that? Roughly speaking, by demonstrating 4 skills:

- How well you can **pick out** words and phrases and list them;
- How well you can write about **the effect** certain words and phrases have on the reader;
- How well you can write about how t**he structure** of the writing adds to the effect of the words on the reader (things like sentence length and so on);
- How well you're able to **use evidence** from the passage to **back up (or contradict)** a statement about the text.

4 questions, all worth differing amounts:

- Question 1 is worth 4 marks

- Questions 2 and 3 are worth 8 marks each
- Question 4 is worth 20 marks

As before, remember that you're looking at about one minute per mark. So 4 minutes on question 1 and 20 minutes on question 4.

If you're 30 minutes into the exam and you're not yet on question 4? Get onto question 4. As 100% of 20 marks is worth a lot more than 50% of 8 marks. Do you follow? Of course you do.

One thing before we start. For every single question, make sure you understand exactly what it's asking you to do (yes, I know I repeat myself a lot, but there's a reason).

I'd suggest underlining the key word or words in the question, to make sure that every sentence you write links back to these key words.

We'll see this in action later when we go through some answers in detail.

QUESTION 1

We want this one over and done with asap as it's worth a measly 4 marks. Let's look at the question from the 2017 exam:

> Read again the first part of the source, from lines 1 to 5.
>
> List four things about Rosabel from this part of the source.
>
> [4 marks]

Remember: look carefully at the question and underline the key word or words:

Read again the first part of the source, from lines 1 to 5.

> List <u>four things about Rosabel</u> from this part of the source.
>
> [4 marks]

Now you're going to read only the part they ask you to: lines 1-5:

> At the corner of Oxford Circus, Rosabel bought a bunch of violets, and that was practically the reason why she had so little tea – for a scone and a boiled egg and a cup of cocoa are not

sufficient after a hard day's work in a hat shop. As she swung onto the step of the bus, grabbed her skirt with one hand and clung to the railing with the other, Rosabel thought she would have sacrificed her soul for a good dinner, something hot and strong and filling.

Take your trusty pen (you don't need highlighters in a million colours, trust me. A pen will do) and underline 4 words or phrases that tell us something about Rosabel:

At the corner of Oxford Circus, Rosabel bought a <u>bunch of violets</u>, and that was practically the reason why she had so little tea – for <u>a scone and a boiled egg and a cup of cocoa are not sufficient after a hard day's work in a hat shop</u>. As she <u>swung onto the step of the bus</u>, grabbed her skirt with one hand and <u>clung to the railing with the other</u>, Rosabel thought <u>she would have sacrificed her soul for a good dinner</u>, something hot and strong and filling.

Plenty there to be going on with.

When you come to list, make sure what you list makes sense. You are able to either quote directly, or paraphrase (in other words, change the quote a bit to show you understand what it tells us about Rosabel):

1. She bought a bunch of violets
2. She had a scone, boiled egg and cup of cocoa for tea
3. She had been working hard in a hat shop
4. She swung onto the steps of the bus

And so on. There are least another 4 available.

And that's it. Question 1 done. Hopefully no more than 4-5 minutes, remember…

QUESTION 2

OK, this is where the road starts to get bumpier. As this question is asking you to explain, **in your own words**, about the writer creates particular effects - in other words, how the writer is trying to make you feel certain things about the subject.

Don't worry if you actually feel nothing other than the icy grip of exam panic: imagine what the writer is trying to communicate to the average reader.

You'll notice below that I go into a fair bit of detail: possibly more than your teachers did. That's not to criticise your teachers in any way: they probably didn't have time to do this - I know I didn't when I was in the classroom. But it's worthwhile taking the time to understand the nuts and bolts of each question.

Think of it like learning a series of recipes before you go on Masterchef: it will help you to visualise the steps you need to take to ensure you nail the meringue when you're on camera. Mmmm, meringue…

Sorry, on to the question:

> Look in detail at this extract, from lines 6 to 14 of the source:

> Rosabel looked out of the windows; the street was blurred and misty, but light striking on the panes turned their dullness to opal and silver, and the jewellers' shops seen through this were fairy palaces. Her feet were horribly wet, and she knew the bottom of her skirt and petticoat would be coated with black, greasy mud. There was a sickening smell of warm humanity – it seemed to be oozing out of everybody in the bus – and everybody had the same expression, sitting so still, staring in front of them. Rosabel stirred suddenly and unfastened the two top buttons of her coat... she felt almost stifled. Through her half-closed eyes, the whole row of people on the opposite seat seemed to resolve into one meaningless, staring face.
>
> How does the writer use language here to describe Rosabel's bus journey home? You could include the writer's choice of:
>
> words and phrases
>
> language features and techniques
>
> sentence forms.
>
> [8 marks]

As I think I may have mentioned earlier, use those three bullet points. USE THOSE THREE BULLET POINTS (that's me shouting, but not in an aggressive, bullying way, but more in a 'come on you can do it' sports coach sort of way).

I think they should say 'you must include' or 'if you don't include you'll lose marks'. At least that would be honest.

Make sure you read that question again and underline the key words:

> How does the writer use <u>language</u> here to describe <u>Rosabel's bus journey home</u>?

So, let's use the above bullet points and focus our attention only on that journey home and nothing else.

Remember: 8 minutes on this question. I'd suggest 2-3 minutes reading, underlining and jotting down a few quick notes, and 5-6 minutes answering

This means only one paragraph. Not three paragraphs. And did I mention you should refer to those bullet points? Just checking.

Let's see what we might underline in the passage:

> Rosabel looked out of the windows; the street was blurred and misty, but light striking on the panes turned their dullness to <u>opal and silver</u>, and the jewellers' shops seen through this were <u>fairy palaces</u>. Her feet were horribly wet, and she knew the bottom of her skirt and petticoat would be coated with black, greasy mud. There was a <u>sickening smell of warm humanity</u> – it seemed to be oozing out of everybody in the bus – and <u>everybody had the same expression</u>, sitting so still, staring in front of them. Rosabel stirred suddenly and unfastened the two top buttons of her coat... <u>she felt almost stifled</u>. Through her half-closed eyes, the whole row of people on the opposite seat seemed to resolve into one <u>meaningless, staring face</u>.

Quite a lot there, so it shouldn't be too hard to turn this into a paragraph.

Now, rather than getting started on the answer straight away, take a minute to jot down some impressions. I'd suggest doing this beside the extract, where you've underlined things.

What you're looking for is the general feeling of the journey the passage gives, and how Rosabel feels about it.

What strikes me when I read this is the contrast between the world outside the bus, and the world inside. Outside seems such a magical place, but inside it's pretty grim. So, I start to jot notes down, just a few words and phrases:

- Street seems magical and dreamlike - opal, silver, fairy palaces

- Inside contrast - sickening, oozing - negative description of people
- Rosabel feels stifled
- Meaningless - pointless existence

That sort of thing - just quick impressions which should take a minute or so. What you're doing is dumping ideas down that you can then turn into your answer.

What's important here is that you're not just writing down quotes - you're making notes on the effect they have on the reader.

Now, let's look at a couple of different answers and explore how they differ. We'll start with a solid, grade 5-6 answer.

THE GRADE 5-6 APPROACH

For a solid, grade 5-6 answer, you want to make sure you use quotes and explain how they answer the question. I know this sounds obvious, but it's amazing how easy it is to forget to quote when you're under pressure.

Quotes can, and should, be either individual words or very short phrases - don't quote whole long sentences as this wastes time and doesn't show you able to lift the relevant stuff from the extract and dump the rest.

Here's the example 5-6 mark answer from the examiner's mark scheme. It's not the whole answer but it gives you a good idea about what the examiner will be looking for when they mark your exam:

> The writer uses positive language to describe the view from the bus on Rosabel's journey home. The jewellers' shops are 'fairy palaces', an image to suggest that the light shining on the steamed-up bus windows makes the buildings sparkle and appear dream-like and magical to Rosabel. However, negative language is then used to portray the stuffy atmosphere inside the bus. She says the people 'seemed to resolve into one meaningless, staring face', a metaphor to imply that everyone looks alike and blurs into one

dull, ordinary group going about their pointless, everyday lives. In this way, the writer's use of language contrasts Rosabel's imaginary world outside the bus with what her life is really like.

Let's take a moment to pick this apart and see how it works. As you can see, it's really not bad: and this should give you an indication as to the level you need to be writing at in order to get a decent grade.

Don't let this put you off: you can practise this technique until you can apply it easily under pressure.

So, in the above example we have:

- A couple of quotes;
- Some language which shows the writer is able to explain: 'to suggest that', 'used to portray', 'to imply that';
- Some technical language: 'image', 'metaphor', 'contrasts'.

In a nutshell, three things: **quote, explain, use the right language**. Oh, and ensure every quote and explanation answers the question.

It is that simple when you break it down. Trust me!

AIMING HIGHER: GRADES 7 AND ABOVE

Now, I'll level with you. As I think we've got off to a good start so I wouldn't want to fool you or get you thinking that if you follow this guide to the letter you're guaranteed a top grade. Life ain't like that.

The really top marks (8 and 9) are hard to teach. Some students just seem to have that bit extra. You may be one of those people. If you are, thanks for reading this, and I hope some of it helps, but you're probably less in need of my help than others.

I'm not saying that following my advice won't help you reach those very top grades: it's just that following a formula can only get you so far.

There's a flair, an originality, to the highest graded answers that most teachers would say is beyond their ability to teach.

What any good teacher should do is create good foundations and give students the confidence to really go for it and show what they're capable of. Some might disagree - but it's always been my philosophy and did the kids I taught pretty well.

Having said all that, there's nothing wrong in looking at how the top answers are constructed so you know the ingredients and can apply them in your own exam.

Remember: playing the game is what it's all about. The top students just seem to instinctively know this better than others. Lucky them!

Let's now look at an example of a top graded answer. Again, not the whole answer, but enough for us to see what they're doing differently from the 5-6 answer.

Don't be intimidated by this: it's been written by an examiner and is to be used as a guide for those marking the exams. But once we break it down we can see that it's not much different from the 5-6 answer - it just has more of the good stuff:

> The writer employs very different language to describe the view from the bus and the claustrophobic, mundane atmosphere within it. As the light catches the misty window panes, jewellers' shops are transformed into 'fairy palaces' for Rosabel. Metaphorically, these shops symbolise a dream-like fantasy world full of sparkle, magic and enchantment, a world that is completely unobtainable for a lower class shop girl like her. However, the passengers inside the bus are described collectively as 'one meaningless, staring face', suggesting their features are indistinguishable: they have blurred into a single anonymous being that personifies the hollow, pointless existence that seems to be their lives. In the bus journey home, the writer's use of language contrasts the outside world of Rosabel's hopes and dreams with the inside reality of her life.

This answer does a couple of things differently from the first answer we looked at:

1. Language and sentence structure are more sophisticated;
2. The analysis is much deeper and shows sparks of originality.

That's it. It's not doing anything incredible or impossible. It's just using a broader vocabulary, more complex sentences, and shows the candidate has thought deeply about the effect of the language on the reader.

Let's break it down in the same way we did the 5-6 answer. What we see is:

- Well-chosen quotes throughout, that feed nicely into the sentence (more on this technique later);
- The explicit use of sophisticated language: 'employs', 'metaphorically', 'symbolise', 'collectively', 'contrasts';
- Linking words to show either the development of an idea, or to indicate contrast: 'However';
- The use of a colon to indicate that explanation (analysis) will follow: 'indistinguishable: they have blurred...';
- A final, short and clear summing up of what's just been explored: 'the writer's use of language contrasts the outside world....'.

See? Really not that different from the first example, but with a bit more sugar in the meringue.

YOUR TURN!

Still not convinced you can do it yourself? I don't believe you. Let's look at another example and work through it together. Don't worry: I've got your back.

We'll look at the opening of a book you may know already. It's *Of Mice and Men*, by John Steinbeck.

> Look in detail at the extract from the opening of Of Mice and Men:
>
> A few miles south of Soledad, the Salinas River drops in close to the hillside bank and runs deep and green. The water is warm too, for it has slipped twinkling over the yellow sands in the sunlight before reaching the narrow pool. On one side of the river the golden foothill slopes curve up to the strong and rocky Gabilan Mountains, but on the valley side the water is lined with trees-willows fresh and green with every spring, carrying in their lower leaf junctures the debris of the winter's flooding; and sycamores with mottled, white, recumbent limbs and branches that arch over the pool. On the sandy bank under the trees the leaves lie deep and so crisp that a lizard makes a great skittering if he runs among them. Rabbits come out of the brush to sit on the sand in the

evening, and the damp flats are covered with the night tracks of 'coons, and with the spread pads of dogs from the ranches, and with the split-wedge tracks of deer that come to drink in the dark.

How does the writer use language to describe the natural world?

You could include the writer's choice of:

Words and phrases

Language features and techniques

Sentence forms

OK: you're going to start by taking your pen and:

1. Underline the key words in the question that will focus your answer;
2. Underline any words and phrases in the extract which refer to the natural world.

Have a go at underlining the above before moving on. If you're using the Kindle version use the Kindle highlighter.

Here's my underlined extract:

> A few miles south of Soledad, the Salinas River drops in close to the hillside bank and runs <u>deep and green</u>. The <u>water is warm</u> too, for it has slipped <u>twinkling over the yellow sands</u> in the sunlight before reaching the narrow pool. On one side of the river the <u>golden foothill slopes</u> curve up to the <u>strong and rocky Gabilan Mountains</u>, but on the valley side the water is lined with trees- willows <u>fresh and green</u> with every spring, carrying in their lower leaf junctures the debris of the winter's flooding; and sycamores with <u>mottled, white, recumbent limbs</u> and branches that arch over the pool. On the sandy bank under the trees the <u>leaves lie deep and so crisp</u> that a <u>lizard makes a great skittering</u> if he runs among them. Rabbits come out of the brush to sit on the sand in the evening, and the <u>damp flats are covered with the night tracks of 'coons</u>, and with the spread pads of dogs from the

ranches, and with the split-wedge tracks of deer that come to drink in the dark.

As before, we want to think about the overall impression we get, and any contrasts we see being developed.

A SIMPLE THREE STEP FORMULA

Now, when you write your response keep in mind there's a particular order in which we write things. We've already seen that with the other answers but haven't looked closely at it so far. It's something like this:

1. Language feature
2. Quote
3. Effect (analysis)

I'll show you below what I mean. When you look closely, all our answers are doing is referring to quotes and explaining how they answer the question. The more you do this, the easier it gets.

And when it's second nature you'll find yourself saying more interesting things, seeing patterns developing, testing out ideas, having original insights.

If you don't know how to approach writing the basic answer you'll struggle to access the higher marks. Like trying to make a meringue without knowing how to break an egg. And no, I'm not obsessed with meringues.

Have a go at writing an answer before looking at my example.

MY SAMPLE GRADE 7-8 ANSWER

Here's my examiner-style model answer. I've tried not to be too show-offy, but you may as well see the sort of quality Jeff and Jane will be looking for whilst sipping their flat white:

The opening sentence of the passage uses the adjectives 'deep' and 'green' to introduce the beautiful, calm natural world of Salinas. This is furthered by the rich, evocative alliteration of 'the water is warm' and the onomatopoeic verb 'twinkling': the sounds of these words have a calming effect on the reader, as if by reading them they can both hear and feel the stillness of the place. The following complex sentence builds one image on top of another, suggesting there is almost too much beauty to take in: the 'strong and rocky… mountains' contrasting with the 'fresh and green' willows. The final complex sentence brings animals into this natural world: the repetition of the animals' 'tracks' and 'pads' suggestive of their repetition on the ground, developed further by the monosyllabic choice which has a hypnotic effect on the reader.

As you can see, I have tried to cram as much possible into this short answer, but I did this for a reason. I wanted to show you how using this strict three stage formula enables you to say some interest things whilst always keeping within a tight structure.

We can look carefully at one sentence (bold italics) and break it down further:

- ***This is furthered by the rich, evocative alliteration of***
- Introduce the language form - in this case 'alliteration'
- ***'the water is warm' and the onomatopoeic verb 'twinkling'***
- The quotes, with a further language technique 'onomatopoeia'
- ***the sounds of these words have a calming effect on the reader, as if by reading them they can both hear and feel the stillness of the place.***
- An explanation of the quotes' effect on the reader.

Note how this sentence uses a colon to introduce the explanation/analysis. I always referred to these as 'analytical signposts' to my students: in other words, you are explicitly showing the examiner that some explanation/analysis is coming up. Never a bad thing.

You'll also see that I referred to language techniques we normally refer to in poetry - alliteration, onomatopoeia.

Never be scared to use the stuff you've learnt in poetry analysis when answering language exam questions. Novelists use these as much as poets.

QUESTION 3

Now, on to the first 'whole passage' question, which is pretty tough considering it's worth only 8 marks:

> You now need to think about the whole of the source.
>
> This text is from the beginning of a short story.
>
> How has the writer structured the text to interest you as a reader? You could write about:
>
> what the writer focuses your attention on at the beginning of the source
>
> how and why the writer changes this focus as the source develops
>
> any other structural features that interest you.
>
> [8 marks]

When you underline the key words above (which you are now doing without thinking), you can see that the question is asking you to focus on **structure**. This is key: it's all about **how the passage is constructed** to hold your interest throughout.

43

This is quite tough, but we will break it down so you can see how you'd approach a question like this should it come up in the exam. Which is highly likely.

What you are going to look for are the techniques the writer uses to focus your attention on certain bits, and how they make you read quickly or more slowly depending on how they use punctuation, sentence length, punctuation and so on. You're also going to focus on how contrasts are used.

Remember: 8 marks. The same as question 2. So don't spend hours on this one. No more than 10 minutes is my advice.

And guess what: that's right. Use the bullet points as a guide. No need for me to shout at you this time. As before, underline anything that stands out and make notes in the margin.

Here's the passage:

> At the corner of Oxford Circus, Rosabel bought a bunch of violets, and that was practically the reason why she had so little tea – for a scone and a boiled egg and a cup of cocoa are not sufficient after a hard day's work in a hat shop. As she swung onto the step of the bus, grabbed her skirt with one hand and clung to the railing with the other, Rosabel thought she would have sacrificed her soul for a good dinner, something hot and strong and filling.
>
> Rosabel looked out of the windows; the street was blurred and misty, but light striking on the panes turned their dullness to opal and silver, and the jewellers' shops seen through this were fairy palaces. Her feet were horribly wet, and she knew the bottom of her skirt and petticoat would be coated with black, greasy mud. There was a sickening smell of warm humanity – it seemed to be oozing out of everybody in the bus – and everybody had the same expression, sitting so still, staring in front of them. Rosabel stirred suddenly and unfastened the two top buttons of her coat... she felt almost stifled. Through her half-closed eyes, the whole row of

people on the opposite seat seemed to resolve into one meaningless, staring face.

She began to think of all that had happened during the day. Would she ever forget that awful woman in the grey mackintosh, or the girl who had tried on every hat in the shop and then said she would 'call in tomorrow and decide definitely'? Rosabel could not help smiling; the excuse was worn so thin.

But there had been one other – a girl with beautiful red hair and a white skin and eyes the colour of that green ribbon shot with gold they had got from Paris last week. Rosabel had seen her carriage at the door; a man had come in with her, quite a young man, and so well dressed.

'What is it exactly that I want, Harry?' she had said, as Rosabel took the pins out of her hat, untied her veil, and gave her a hand-mirror.

'You must have a black hat,' he had answered, 'a black hat with a feather that goes right round it and then round your neck and ties in a bow under your chin – and a decent-sized feather.'

The girl glanced at Rosabel laughingly. 'Have you any hats like that?'

They had been very hard to please; Harry would demand the impossible, and Rosabel was almost in despair. Then she remembered the big, untouched box upstairs.

'Oh, one moment, Madam,' she had said. 'I think perhaps I can show you something that will please you better.' She had run up, breathlessly, cut the cords, scattered the tissue paper, and yes, there was the very hat – rather large, soft, with a great, curled feather, and a black velvet rose, nothing else. They had been charmed. The girl had put it on and then handed it to Rosabel.

'Let me see how it looks on you,' she said. Rosabel turned to the mirror and placed it on her brown hair, then faced them.

'Oh, Harry, isn't it adorable,' the girl cried, 'I must have that!' She smiled again at Rosabel. 'It suits you, beautifully.'

A sudden, ridiculous feeling of anger had seized Rosabel. She longed to throw the lovely, perishable thing in the girl's face, and bent over the hat, flushing.

'It's exquisitely finished off inside, Madam,' she said. The girl swept out to her carriage, and left Harry to pay and bring the box with him.

'I shall go straight home and put it on before I come out to lunch with you,' Rosabel heard her say.

The biggest challenge here is to take quite a long passage and find the main points to write a short paragraph or two. It's tempting to go through the whole thing and explain paragraph by paragraph - but that would take too long and you're in danger of not having enough time for the more important final question.

So, what you do is this. Think about the passage as you would a movie, and think of the writer like the movie's director:

- Where is the 'camera' at the opening? Is it a wide shot of the whole scene? Does it focus on small details? Is it a closer up shot of a person? Are we drawn to detail or given a bigger picture?
- Where does the camera move to next? The same scene, only closer?
- How are characters introduced? Do we get a description of them or do they just start speaking?
- How is the passage of time shown? In a film, directors often use a fade from one scene to the next. Is there any equivalent in the passage?
- Think of the punctuation a bit like you might consider how a film is edited. In the same way that a film might cut from one character and scene to the next to build speed, so a writer might use commas rather than lots of full stops to

show speed, and slow the writing down by bringing in more full stops and colons.

THE GRADE 5-6 APPROACH

Let's have a look at the example grade 5-6 answer to see what we mean.

> At the beginning the writer focuses our attention on the thoughts of Rosabel, who is travelling home 'after a hard day's work in a hat shop'. We learn that she would have 'sacrificed her soul for a good dinner', so this immediately establishes the main character as a lower class girl who is poor and hungry, despite how hard she works. We then shift in time as Rosabel experiences a flashback to 'all that had happened during the day', with the focus narrowing to her serving a 'girl with beautiful red hair'. In the final line of their exchange, the girl tells her boyfriend she is going to wear her new hat when 'I come out to lunch with you'. This reminds us of the beginning when Rosabel was hungry, so the structure emphasises how very different the two girls are.

You can see how they even use the language of film: 'focuses', 'focus narrowing', 'flashback'. This is a good idea as it keeps you writing about structure rather than the effect of language.

What else does it do?

- It takes the passage in order: 'At the beginning', 'We then shift in time', 'In the final line';
- It uses quotes to indicate which part of the passage it's referring to;
- It uses the same technique as before - introduce, quote, explain.

However, this answer seems quite 'surface' and is probably a bit too short for the higher grades. You need to look more closely for those top grades. Let's see an example.

THE GRADE 7 AND ABOVE APPROACH

As you'll see from the below, there are similarities with the above - but we're more interested in the differences as this will help us unlock those higher grades:

> At the beginning the writer focuses on the private thoughts of Rosabel who is travelling home 'after a hard day's work in a hat shop'. Her social situation is immediately established as we learn she would have 'sacrificed her soul for a good dinner': she is poor, hungry and lower class. Time is then used as a structural feature as Rosabel experiences a flashback to 'all that had happened during the day', and the focus narrows as she reflects specifically on serving a 'girl with beautiful red hair'. The rest of the text involves the reader in the directness of their exchange through dialogue, and we witness Rosabel's public persona of a subservient shop girl in real time. Rosabel's external actions in this section, together with her earlier, more private, internal thoughts, now provide the reader with a fully rounded character. In the final line, the red-haired girl tells her boyfriend she is going to wear her new hat when 'I come out to lunch with you,' which takes us back to the beginning when Rosabel could not afford a decent meal. This circular structure manipulates the reader into favouring Rosabel,

and possibly disliking the red- haired girl for her privilege and wealth.

Let's look carefully at what it's doing:

- It goes in order of events, like the other answer;
- It has a greater command of language: 'immediately established', 'structural feature', 'reflects specifically', 'public persona';
- Specific reference to the reader: 'we learn she', 'involves the reader', 'provide the reader', 'manipulates the reader';
- Quotes feeding nicely into each sentence;
- Excellent use of punctuation:
- a colon to explain - ': she is poor, hungry and lower class'
- commas to show analysis building up - 'Rosabel's external actions in this section, together with her earlier, more private, internal thoughts…'
- Use of language suggesting a testing of ideas: 'and possibly disliking the red-haired girl'.

Of all of these, the last one is one of the key differentiators of the top answers from the less-so. By using words like 'possibly', 'seems to suggest' and 'might', you show that you are testing ideas, exploring the motivations of the writer without nailing it down to definites.

After all, this is fiction writing - there is a lot of room for movement.

51

YOUR TURN!

Let's look back at the opening of 'Of Mice and Men'. This time a little more of the passage:

> A few miles south of Soledad, the Salinas River drops in close to the hillside bank and runs deep and green. The water is warm too, for it has slipped twinkling over the yellow sands in the sunlight before reaching the narrow pool. On one side of the river the golden foothill slopes curve up to the strong and rocky Gabilan Mountains, but on the valley side the water is lined with trees- willows fresh and green with every spring, carrying in their lower leaf junctures the debris of the winter's flooding; and sycamores with mottled, white, recumbent limbs and branches that arch over the pool. On the sandy bank under the trees the leaves lie deep and so crisp that a lizard makes a great skittering if he runs among them. Rabbits come out of the brush to sit on the sand in the evening, and the damp flats are covered with the night tracks of 'coons, and with the spread pads of dogs from the ranches, and with the split-wedge tracks of deer that come to drink in the dark.
>
> There is a path through the willows and among the sycamores, a path beaten hard by boys coming down from the ranches to swim

in the deep pool, and beaten hard by tramps who come wearily down from the highway in the evening to jungle-up near water. In front of the low horizontal limb of a giant sycamore there is an ash pile made by many fires; the limb is worn smooth by men who have sat on it.

Evening of a hot day started the little wind to moving among the leaves. The shade climbed up the hills toward the top. On the sand banks the rabbits sat as quietly as little gray sculptured stones. And then from the direction of the state highway came the sound of footsteps on crisp sycamore leaves. The rabbits hurried noiselessly for cover. A stilted heron labored up into the air and pounded down river. For a moment the place was lifeless, and then two men emerged from the path and came into the opening by the green pool.

We are looking at the structure of the passage and how it interests the reader. Go through the above carefully, making notes on how the writer directs our attention as we read through the passage. Remember our film director technique: this passage works really well for this.

- Where do we start? Wide? Narrow?
- How are details introduced?
- How does the 'camera' move through the scene?
- How does it focus in on certain parts of the scene?

Have a go at writing an answer before comparing with the one below.

Here's a possible (part) answer:

> The passage opens with the general location: 'a few miles south of Soledad'. From here, the writer draws the reader's attention to the river: the fact that it 'drops' and 'runs' focuses us on its movement and draws us into the scene. We are then drawn to the contrast between one side of the valley and the other by the conjunction 'but': this suggests that this is an environment of contrast. The

writer then focuses our attention onto smaller details: first, the 'sycamores', then their 'branches', then the 'leaves'. We feel as if we are moving further into the scene, taking in smaller and smaller details. This is further emphasised by the repetition of the animals' tracks, as our attention moves from the level of the mountains to the ground where the animals live.

…and so on.

I hope you can see what I've done here. I've focused continually on where the writer is placing our attention, and why. This is vital for the higher marks. I could have listed how the writer moves us into the scene, but unless I'd said why he does this I would only have got around 5 marks.

QUESTION 4

This is the big one. The one you should spend a full 20 minutes on. Not the one you rush through because you took too long on questions 1-3 (I really cannot stress this enough).

This question asks you to state your opinion on a fictional statement by a fictional student, using evidence from the text to back up your point of view.

Now, you have three ways of going about this. You can either agree with the statement, disagree with it, or have a mixed response.

My suggestion would be to go for the third approach: to remain sufficiently open to find evidence that backs up the student's comment, but also look for ways you could argue the opposite.

Here's question 4:

> Focus this part of your answer on the second part of the source, from line 19 to the end.
>
> A student said, 'This part of the story, set in the hat shop, shows that the red-haired girl has many advantages in life, and I think Rosabel is right to be angry.'

To what extent do you agree? In your response, you could:

consider your own impressions of the red-haired girl

evaluate how the writer conveys Rosabel's reactions to the red-haired girl

support your response with references to the text.

[20 marks]

(Perhaps it should actually start: 'No student said ever'. But what do I know?)

First of all, read through the question and underline the important bits:

- Line 19 to the end
- The red-haired girl has many advantages in life
- Rosabel has a right to be angry
- How much do you agree?

Let's look back at the last section of the passage:

> But there had been one other – a girl with beautiful red hair and a white skin and eyes the colour of that green ribbon shot with gold they had got from Paris last week. Rosabel had seen her carriage at the door; a man had come in with her, quite a young man, and so well dressed.
>
> 'What is it exactly that I want, Harry?' she had said, as Rosabel took the pins out of her hat, untied her veil, and gave her a hand-mirror.
>
> 'You must have a black hat,' he had answered, 'a black hat with a feather that goes right round it and then round your neck and ties in a bow under your chin – and a decent-sized feather.'
>
> The girl glanced at Rosabel laughingly. 'Have you any hats like that?'

They had been very hard to please; Harry would demand the impossible, and Rosabel was almost in despair. Then she remembered the big, untouched box upstairs.

'Oh, one moment, Madam,' she had said. 'I think perhaps I can show you something that will please you better.' She had run up, breathlessly, cut the cords, scattered the tissue paper, and yes, there was the very hat – rather large, soft, with a great, curled feather, and a black velvet rose, nothing else. They had been charmed. The girl had put it on and then handed it to Rosabel.

'Let me see how it looks on you,' she said. Rosabel turned to the mirror and placed it on her brown hair, then faced them.

'Oh, Harry, isn't it adorable,' the girl cried, 'I must have that!' She smiled again at Rosabel. 'It suits you, beautifully.'

A sudden, ridiculous feeling of anger had seized Rosabel. She longed to throw the lovely, perishable thing in the girl's face, and bent over the hat, flushing.

'It's exquisitely finished off inside, Madam,' she said. The girl swept out to her carriage, and left Harry to pay and bring the box with him.

'I shall go straight home and put it on before I come out to lunch with you,' Rosabel heard her say.

When it comes to this answer, one thing is worth stating from the off. Quantity doesn't always mean quality. Just because it's worth 20 marks, doesn't mean you have to write 20 pages.

Remember my point about Jeff and Jane - they have *so many* of these exams to mark. Do them a favour and keep it tightly focused.

My advice is therefore to spend 8-10 minutes carefully reading and making notes, and 10-12 minutes writing the answer. Remember: your focus is on whether you agree that Rosabel should be angry with the red-haired girl's advantages.

As before, ensure all the notes you make refer to those three bullet points - your own impressions, how the writer conveys Rosabel's reactions, and quotes. You can make notes on the passage itself or on your answer paper - there is no right or wrong way of doing this.

This answer is less about specific language techniques or structural choices (unless they help you to explore Rosabel's point of view). It's more about how well you use quotes to argue for/against the student's statement.

Let's turn to the sample answers to see how they tackle this question. Again - not necessarily a whole answer, but enough for us to see what's going on and how they differ.

A GRADE 5-6 ANSWER

Here's the sample answer:

> The red-haired girl does seem to have many advantages in life. She arrives in a carriage to go hat shopping, which tells us she's wealthy, and she has a 'well- dressed' boyfriend, all outward signs of success. She is also attractive, and the writer uses colour to imply how alive and vibrant she is: 'beautiful red hair and a white skin and eyes the colour of that green ribbon shot with gold'. She has everything that Rosabel doesn't have, and I think this makes Rosabel jealous because she recognises how unfair life is. However, the girl isn't unpleasant so I'm not sure that Rosabel is right to get annoyed. When Rosabel tries on the hat, her anger is 'sudden' and 'ridiculous', adjectives that show her reaction is unexpected and ultimately silly because there's nothing she can do about the girl having all these advantages and her having none.

Let's see what it's doing well:

- It begins by suggesting agreement with the student - but by using 'seems' keeps opinions open;

- There is some explanation signposted by phrase like 'which tells us that' and 'to imply how';
- It uses quotes fluently, feeding them into each sentence;
- It indicates disagreement with the statement by the use of 'However' and 'I'm not sure that'.

All solid and well written. But when we look at the 7-8 answer we can see where the differences lie.

A GRADE 7 AND ABOVE ANSWER

Let's see the contrast with the answer above:

> Although Rosabel's anger is understandable, it is not entirely justified, even though the red-haired girl does appear to have many advantages in life. She has wealth, beauty and happiness, all characteristics of a privileged lifestyle, and the writer's use of colour to describe her - 'beautiful red hair and a white skin and eyes the colour of that green ribbon shot with gold' - implies she is also radiant, vivacious and exotic. This is in direct contrast to the brown-haired Rosabel, who can only dream of being like this.
>
> I think Rosabel is envious and maybe even resentful, which is why her anger is understandable. When Rosabel tries on the hat, the key sentence 'Let me see how it looks on you,' is significant because, just for one moment, their lives overlap. In a way, Rosabel is being taunted with a symbol of another, much better life, but this is not deliberate, which is why her 'sudden, ridiculous feeling of anger' is not really fair on the girl. The adjective 'sudden' implies the fury comes out of nowhere, as if Rosabel has no control over it, and 'ridiculous' suggests it is unreasonable to the point of being absurd. The girl does have many of life's

advantages, but she is a product of her upbringing in much the same way as Rosabel, and is not to blame for the class divisions in society.

So what's different?

- It immediately asserts a point of view: 'not entirely justified'. Note the use of the word 'entirely', which allows this student to explore both points of view;
- It uses a clever technique to introduce a longer quote into the sentence - notice the dashes in the second sentence. This are a type of parentheses, like brackets, and separate out the quote from its introduction and its analysis. You can use brackets as well here - but the dashes work well;
- Lots of intelligent analytical language: 'implies', 'key sentence', 'significant', 'suggests';
- Language which shows the student trying out different possiblities: 'I think', 'maybe', 'In a way', 'as if';
- A final summary sentence, showing the examiner that the student is able to draw their points to a logical close.

It wouldn't be hard to get more than 16 marks with this answer. Jeff would be a happy man if he read this. His pulse would lower and he'd not need to reach for the chocolate chip cookies. See? You're helping him with his blood pressure by writing something this clear and clean. Good for you!

YOUR TURN!

Let's turn our attention back to our friend Mr Steinbeck, and his wonderful novel *Of Mice and Men*. We'll look at the next section, which turns our attention to the two men:

> They had walked in single file down the path, and even in the open one stayed behind the other. Both were dressed in denim trousers and in denim coats with brass buttons. Both wore black, shapeless hats and both carried tight blanket rolls slung over their shoulders. The first man was small and quick, dark of face, with restless eyes and sharp, strong features. Every part of him was defined: small, strong hands, slender arms, a thin and bony nose. Behind him walked his opposite, a huge man, shapeless of face, with large, pale eyes, and wide, sloping shoulders; and he walked heavily, dragging his feet a little, the way a bear drags his paws. His arms did not swing at his sides, but hung loosely.
>
> The first man stopped short in the clearing, and the follower nearly ran over him. He took off his hat and wiped the sweat-band with his forefinger and snapped the moisture off. His huge companion dropped his blankets and flung himself down and drank from the surface of the green pool; drank with long gulps,

snorting into the water like a horse. The small man stepped nervously beside him.

"Lennie!" he said sharply. "Lennie, for God' sakes don't drink so much." Lennie continued to snort into the pool. The small man leaned over and shook him by the shoulder. "Lennie. You gonna be sick like you was last night."

Lennie dipped his whole head under, hat and all, and then he sat up on the bank and his hat dripped down on his blue coat and ran down his back. "That's good," he said. "You drink some, George. You take a good big drink." He smiled happily.

George unslung his bindle and dropped it gently on the bank. "I ain't sure it's good water," he said. "Looks kinda scummy."

Lennie dabbled his big paw in the water and wiggled his fingers so the water arose in little splashes; rings widened across the pool to the other side and came back again. Lennie watched them go. "Look, George. Look what I done."

George knelt beside the pool and drank from his hand with quick scoops. "Tastes all right," he admitted. "Don't really seem to be running, though. You never oughta drink water when it ain't running, Lennie," he said hopelessly. "You'd drink out of a gutter if you was thirsty."

Here's the question:

A student, having read this section of the text, said: 'George seems not to trust Lennie, and I think this is unfair'.

To what extent do you agree? In your response, you could:

Consider your own impressions of George and Lennie;

Evaluate how the writer convey's George's reactions to Lennie;

Support your response with reference to the text.

[20 marks]

Remember our technique: we'll spend 6-8 minutes reading through and making notes, and 10-12 minutes writing the answer. As you read it through, look carefully at how Lennie's character is introduced and why George might react in the way he does to Lennie's actions.

Now, have a go at writing the answer. Use the previous Grade 7-8 answer as a model, and try where possible to structure your answer in a similar way.

MY EXAMPLE ANSWER

Here's the start of one I made earlier. See what you think:

> Although George's suspicious attitude towards Lennie may seem unfair at first glance, we can see from the opening passage that there is a reason for this. The contrast between the two men is set up sharply from the start: the first man (George) is 'small and quick' and has 'restless eyes and sharp, strong features', suggesting that he is a naturally wary person, always on the look out for danger. However, the second (Lennie) is 'huge', 'shapeless' and walks 'heavily': he seems far less aware of his surroundings. The fact that the men are introduced one after the other, with the first man leading the second, suggests that the first man is in charge, and is in fact looking after the second. This makes his natural lack of trust more justifiable. When George reacts to Lennie drinking water - "'Lennie, for God's sake don't drink so much.'" - we can see he is doing this out of care for Lennie: he doesn't want him to drink too much and make himself unwell. George is also wary of the environment and can see its potential dangers - he is suspicious of the water as he thinks it 'looks kinda scummy'. We can therefore conclude that George's lack of trust of Lennie is in fact fair: at the end of the day he feels responsible for him so has to look after him as he might a child.

You can probably see how I copied the other answer's structure, and kept to the same 'intro - quote - analysis' structure that you've seen time and again.

I hope all of this has given you enough to go on with. Do remember that the more you practise, the better you get. There are plenty of passages online in the various revision websites that you can use to apply these techniques to.

Remember our Masterchef meringue - practise makes perfect!

PAPER 1 SECTION B

INTRODUCTION

This is the section that many students don't bother to prepare for. However, if you make you sure you tick all the examiner's boxes you'll be a long way ahead of most who take this exam. And let's be honest, you want a higher grade than your friends, don't you? Admit it.

Because this section **is worth the same as the entire section A**. That's right. 40 marks. So if you don't allow yourself enough time here, or write something rubbish, you can undo a lot of the good work you did in section A. And you don't want that, do you.

First of all (and I don't mean to patronise you here) but you do know that YOU ONLY NEED TO ANSWER ONE OF THESE QUESTIONS, NOT TWO. Yes, I knew you knew that. Just checking.

Because I have taught many a foolish student who has in the past ignored my warnings and DONE BOTH. Why? THEY DIDN'T LISTEN TO ME. You can't win 'em all. (OK I've stopped shouting for the time being.)

Let's start by taking a look at the two main areas you'll be assessed on:

- How well you communicate: your writing should be clear and imaginative, and you should use the appropriate language for the purpose and audience of the writing;
- How organised you are, and how well you use spelling, punctuation and grammar to make your writing clear.

So, the writing that will get the top grades will do the following:

- The writing will make the exam marker sit up and take notice (and maybe even spill their coffee);
- It will be matched to its purpose: whether this is description, narrative, argument or persuasion. Each type of writing has different rule/ingredients - make sure you know them;
- It will have excellent vocabulary and use language techniques such as simile and alliteration effectively. Remember that these aren't only for poems;
- It will mix up sentences, with some short and simple, and some long and complex;
- It will link ideas together seamlessly using the correct linking words (like 'however' and 'furthermore');
- It will use paragraphs well, to show ideas progressing fluently;
- Spelling will be (almost) perfect.

I know I've said it before, but it's always worth repeating: make sure every single sentence gets you a mark. Make it interesting. Make it relevant. Use as many techniques as you can (within reason). Mix up sentence types. Link ideas together well with paragraphs.

Simple (ish).

HOW TO WRITE FROM A PHOTO

If we look at the first writing prompt from section B, you will see that you're being asked to respond to a photo. And let's be honest, it's not the most interesting photo ever. Is it.

Hmm.

OK, maybe they'll give you an interesting prompt to get your creative juices flowing:

Describe a journey by bus as suggested by this picture [40 marks]

Nope. That's pretty boring.

Oh well, we just have to make the best of what we have. And actually, it doesn't really matter how boring the photo is, you can make something interesting from it. After all, it's just a hopping off point (sorry about the bus-related pun there).

I'll take you through a four-stage exercise I've done with my students countless times. It will get you exploring the sights, sounds, smells and emotions that can be generated by any image.

Remember it, and use it in the exam. It never fails to make your writing vivid. And, if you jot these notes down on your answer paper before you write, you may even get marks for the ideas if you run out of time and don't get them into the final piece of writing.

This is why you don't want tippex - just one line through with a ruler. Tippex is not your friend. Remember that.

So, here goes. Have your pen at the ready and go through the following exercise:

1. Clear your mind of any first impressions of the photo (e.g. OMG this is so boring etc.)
2. With pen in hand, write down short answers to the following. Just words and short phrases:
3. At least 5 things you can see in the photo, using adjectives wherever possible. For example, *a tired-looking woman looking at the camera, an anxious-looking woman on the phone, neon street lights reflected in the glass, people rushing home from work, the comforting glow of shop windows.*
4. 3-5 things you might here, were you there: *the whine of the bus engine, the swoosh of tyres through a puddle, the stressed voice of the woman on the phone, a baby crying on the top deck, the tinny sound of someone listening to music on headphones.*
5. 3 things you might smell: *someone eating MacDonalds chips, diesel fuel, sickly perfume.*
6. 3-4 emotions that might be present on that bus: *boredom, frustration, loneliness, envy.*

7. You're now going to use these in your description. The trick here is to use these three golden rules:
8. Try to get in as many of the things the examiner is looking for: adjectives, interesting noun and verb choices, similes and metaphors, original ways of describing things and so on.
9. Use different sentence lengths to generate different emotions in the reader. Long sentences are good for flowing description, shorter to build tension and add impact.
10. Paragraph. Paragraph. PARAGRAPH. Key rule: if there is a change of place, time, subject or mood, change paragraph. It's better to have several shorter paragraphs if you're not sure, and it will make your writing easier to read. Which will always please Jeff and Jane.
11. Before you start writing, jot down a brief plan of how you want to structure your answer. It might look something like this:

- Bus's movement, noise, stop and start
- People on the bus, what they might be thinking of
- World outside the bus, contrast with interior.

Notice how this is similar to the passage you've just read? That's not a coincidence. So why not use some of the ideas in your own writing?

SEEING THIS IN ACTION

Let's look at how we might see this in action. You should, if you've been a clever old student and stuck to time in section A, have at least 40-50 minutes for this section, so use this time well.

You're going to use the notes from the exercise as a springboard: as you're writing you'll find new things appearing. That's called creativity and it's what every writer does.

Here's an example few paragraphs:

> The bus makes its stop start way along Oxford Street, a combination of traffic lights and unthinking pedestrians causing the driver to continually hit his brakes, and the passengers on the bus to lurch back and forth as if they are on a boat on rough water. It is December and has been raining all day; the bus's lights glint from the wet black road and its tyres make a swooshing sound as it glides through deepening puddles. For any pedestrians in the way when it passes, they are liable to get soaked.
>
> Celia sits two seats from the front. It is her normal place, as long as no one is sitting there. She likes the womb-like, musty warmth of the bus, especially on a late afternoon like this. She feels protected,

safe, as if nothing could happen to her. Sitting opposite her is a middle-aged woman on the phone: Celia cannot help overhearing her as she complains bitterly down the phone to whoever is listening. Celia guesses either the woman's mother, or a close friend. The woman complains of her job, her lack of money, the fact she hasn't had a holiday all year. Join the club, Celia thinks. She's not alone there.

Remember - you are writing description, so it's all about how vivid and interesting you can make the seemingly mundane.

You don't have to write a story, but you can (and should) bring in a character to make it more personal. Otherwise it can sound a bit dry and lifeless. Having people means having reaction, and that's a good thing.

For a 40-50 minute piece, aim for between 1 and 2 sides. It's better to write less and take your time to make it read well than to write a 10-page masterpiece that looks like it's been written by a drunk spider (or a doctor, which is actually worse).

You may have noticed that I wrote in present tense. There's no rule here: present or past is fine. I just find these shorter descriptive pieces lend themselves quite well to present tense. It's up to you.

YOUR TURN!

Have a look at the photo below and go through the same exercise. I've decided to stay on the theme of journeys for the sake of consistency.

It really doesn't matter what the photo is - you can write about pretty much anything once you've practised. Just go through the exercise and aim for 1-2 sides of A4.

KEY POINTS FROM THE EXAMINER'S MARK SCHEME

This won't differ depending on the photo being used: they're generic pointers that help the examiner to mark your writing.

The grade 5-6 piece of writing will include the following:

- The right style of language for the audience;
- Solid vocabulary and phrasing, chosen for effect and with a range of language techniques;
- Well-structured with clear paragraphs;
- Ideas are connected together well using the right sort of language.
- For the grade 7 and above, you would expect to see:
- Compelling language - the reader will really want to read to the end;
- A sense of assurance - the reader feels confident in the writer and what they're trying to achieve. They don't have to go back and reread sections that aren't immediately clear;
- Variety and inventiveness in structure - such as sentence length and clever use of punctuation;

- Fluently linked paragraphs and seamlessly used connecting language - the whole thing should just flow.

WRITING PROMPT 2

This second prompt will link back into the reading section as well. In this case it's about people from different backgrounds:

> Write a story about two people from different backgrounds.
>
> [40 marks]

Again, not exactly going to set the world on fire, is it. But we can work with this and come up with something interesting.

THE BASIC STRUCTURE OF A STORY

You may have been taught this, but if not it's worth knowing. This is narrative structure at its most basic, but that's all you need to know.

Follow these steps to write a story about pretty much anything, and to ensure it reads well and interests the examiner:

1. You'll need two things first of all - characters and setting. Decide on a main character, and where you'll base the story. I'd suggest you base the story on the point of view of

one character not two. In the above example, it may be two people meeting for the first time.
2. You want to start by placing your main character (MC) in the setting. And get them doing something. Not contemplating the meaning of life. That's boring.
3. Something needs to happen to this character to snap him/her out of his day to day life. In this case it may be meeting this person.
4. This incident sparks a series of events which somehow change the MC. You don't want the MC to be the same at the end as at the beginning.
5. The story reaches a climax where the MC has to make a choice. It shouldn't be easy for them.
6. The story ends with the MC getting back on with their life - only the incident has changed them in some way.

APPLYING IT TO A PROMPT

Applying this to our writing prompt, the notes for the story might be something like this:

1. A young man working in a coffee shop.
2. The man serves a series of unpleasant, arrogant people and hates what he does. He dreams of getting out and doing something with his life.
3. On his way home, he sees a homeless guy being kicked outside the coffee shop and goes to help him.
4. He talks to the homeless man, learns about his background, and decides to help him.
5. The final choice will be whether or not he leaves his job to help this man find his family. He does so, and the man's family turn out to be very wealthy.
6. MC in the coffee shop once more - but this time it is his own, as the family gave him money to thank him.

Yes, it's a bit cheesy, but it has all the ingredients of a compelling story. Have a go writing using these ideas if you wish, or use the narrative structure to think of your own.

You should find it makes writing stories easier.

TIPS FOR EXCELLENT WRITING

Now you've sketched out the structure of the story, use this top tips to help make your writing compelling from start to finish:

1. Use the same sorts of techniques for description that we looked at for the first prompt. No need to go into such depth with planning, but do bring in sights, sounds, smells and emotions. You want to place the reader in the scene from the first sentence. No waffly life philosophy *purlease*.
2. When you imagine your character in the location, get him interacting with it, and with the people around him. Keep it present and concrete throughout. If you find yourself moving into his inner world, get out! It can make the writing very slow.
3. Have an interesting opening - start half way through something happening or someone speaking. Or maybe start by saying 'What I am about to describe is truly shocking. In fact, it is amazing I am here at all to recount these last few days…' Make the reader want to know what's going on.
4. Make sure there is some sort of conflict. In the above story idea, it is the MC's debate as to whether to help the man, the man himself being very different from the MC, and the

MC debating whether to leave his job. Don't have everyone getting on well with one another and it all ending happily as LIFE ISN'T LIKE THAT. Be edgy, dangerous, make the examiner's eyes open a little wider.
5. Remember to mix up sentence length and the rule about paragraphs. Of course. If you forget to paragraph, remember the golden // symbol.

And that's it! With writing, it's all about practise. So don't ignore it - you really do need to make sure you build writing practise into your revision slots. Who knows, you may even find you enjoy creative writing!

I hope so: it's an incredible thing to write well and make other people love what you write.

PAPER 2 SECTION A

PAPER 2: HOW IT DIFFERS FROM PAPER 1

Well done! You survived Paper 1! See, it wasn't so bad, was it. Not once you got inside Jeff's head.

Now on to Paper 2. And, as you might expect, it is in some ways a bit trickier than Paper 1. Even though it has a roughly similar format (reading then writing) there are a few differences worth mentioning:

- The Sources for reading are non-fiction;
- There are two of them;
- They will be from different historical periods;
- For some questions you'll be asked to compare the two Sources;
- You'll produce a piece of non-fiction writing using one starter question.

But don't worry, because there are techniques for answering these questions to get the maximum marks possible. Of course there are!

Remember our mantra: **every single thing you write should get you a mark**. So let's get started with question 1.

SECTION A, QUESTION 1

So, we've spent a few moments reading the front cover and have put away our sparkly purple pen. With our black pen at the ready, we turn the page...

And in the same way as Paper 1, we read only what the question is asking us to read. Yes, we could read the whole thing through, and maybe we'd take some of it in. But maybe not.

So to get these quick 4 marks under our belt why not just read what they tell you to?

Here's the question:

Read again the first part of Source A from lines 1 to 17.

> Choose four statements below which are true.
>
> Shade the circles in the boxes of the ones that you think are true.
>
> Choose a maximum of four statements.
>
> If you make an error cross out the whole box.
>
> If you change your mind and require a statement that has been crossed out then draw a circle around the box.

[4 marks]

1. The writer's son has just had his second birthday.
2. It took a while for the writer to feel close to his son after he was born.
3. The writer has not slept very well over the last year.
4. It takes a long time for the boy to eat his porridge.
5. The writer thinks that his son has grown quickly.
6. The boy has not yet learned to walk.
7. The writer's son knows how to switch off the television.
8. The writer finds it easy to grasp the idea of his son getting older.

What are we being asked to do? Pick out the four true statements about the Source. That's it.

However, it's often not as simple as you might think.

Remember, this is all about you reading closely, so there may be statements that aren't immediately obvious. So be careful, and make sure you check before moving on.

Let's look at the Source from lines 1 to 17:

> My son turned one last week. The day marked the end of what has been both the longest and shortest year of my life. From the instant he was born, it's felt as if my son has always been part of this family. I don't mean that in an obnoxious, heart-eyed, this-was-always-meant-to-be way. I simply mean that I haven't slept for a year and I don't really know how time works any more. Whole years have passed in some of the afternoons I've spent with him lately. Entire galaxies have been born and thrived and withered and died in the time it's taken him to eat a mouthful of porridge.
>
> How is he one already? First he was born, and then I blinked, and now in his place is a little boy who can walk and has teeth and knows how to switch off the television at precisely the most important moment of anything I ever try to watch. It's not exactly the most unprecedented development in all of human history –

child gradually gets older – but it's the first time I've seen it close up. It's honestly quite hard to grasp.

HOW TO ANSWER THIS QUESTION

This is what you do. **You turn each statement into a closed, yes/no question in your head.** Once you've done that, you can find the evidence to answer this question yes or no (funnily enough).

The first statement would then be turned into this question: *Has the writer's son just had his second birthday?* And of course that's wrong - he's just turned one.

On to the second: *Did it take a while for the writer to feel close to his son after he was born?* Again no: it felt like his son had always been part of the family.

And so on. What we then get to is the fact that it's statements C, D, E and G that are true.

Turning statements into questions makes it easy, as it gives you direction.

4 marks. Simple. On to the next!

QUESTION 2

This is where things begin to get harder. Of course they do. Did you really think it was going to be all about choosing a few true statements? You're much cleverer than that.

This question is the first time we are introduced to two different sources: as I said, they'll be on the same topic, but will be from different historical periods.

In the case of the June 2017 exam paper, the topic is childhood.

Now, this is important. Whilst the question does not directly tell you to compare the two texts, **it's worth making reference to any obvious similarities and/or differences when writing the answer**.

There should be obvious ones, and even if you only make one comparison that will increase your marks.

The other thing to mention is that you should **drop in a few quotes**, to show you referring to the text closely.

We'll look at a couple of examples in a moment, just like we did with Paper 1.

Here's the question:

You need to refer to Source A and Source B for this question.

The ways the boys spend their time playing as young children is different.

Use details from both sources to write a summary of the different activities the boy in Source A enjoys and the boy in Source B enjoyed when he was young.

[8 marks]

Here are the two Sources in full:

Source A

This is an article published in The Guardian newspaper in 2016. The writer, Stuart Heritage, explores how he feels now that his son is a year old.

How can my son be a year old already?

He's growing up fast, leaving milestones in his wake – and tiny parts of me along with them

My son turned one last week. The day marked the end of what has been both the longest and shortest year of my life. From the instant he was born, it's felt as if my son has always been part of this family. I don't mean that in an obnoxious, heart-eyed, this-was-always-meant-to-be way. I simply mean that I haven't slept for a year and I don't really know how time works any more. Whole years have passed in some of the afternoons I've spent with him lately. Entire galaxies have been born and thrived and withered and died in the time it's taken him to eat a mouthful of porridge.

How is he one already? First he was born, and then I blinked, and now in his place is a little boy who can walk and has teeth and knows how to switch off the television at precisely the most important moment of anything I ever try to watch. It's not exactly the most unprecedented development in all of human history –

child gradually gets older – but it's the first time I've seen it close up. It's honestly quite hard to grasp.

A year ago, he was a sleepy ball of scrunched-up flesh, but is now determinedly his own person. I can see everyone in him – me, my wife, my parents – yet he's already separate from all of us. He's giddy and silly. He's a show-off, albeit one who's irrationally terrified of my dad. He loves running up to people and waiting for them to twang his lips like a ruler on a table. When he gets tired and barks gibberish in the middle of the room, he throws his entire body into it, like he's trying to shove the noise up a hill.

With every tiny development – every new step he takes, every new tooth and sound and reaction that comes along to ambush us – we're confronted with a slightly different child.

Photos of him taken in the summer seem like dispatches from a million years ago. Photos of him taken last week seem like a different boy. He's blasting ahead as far as he can. He's leaving milestone after milestone in his wake and tiny parts of me along with them.

He'll never again be the tiny baby who nestled in the crook of my arm, sucking on my little finger in the middle of the night while his mum slept. Nor will he be the baby amazed by the taste and texture of solid food. Soon enough he'll stop being the baby who totters over and rests his head on my shoulder whenever he gets tired, or laughs uncontrollably whenever I say the word 'teeth' for reasons I don't think I'll ever work out.

But I've had a year of this and it's ok. He's never going to stop changing, and I don't want him to. This sadness, this constant sense of loss, of time slipping just beyond your grasp, is an important part of this process. He won't realise this, of course. He's got years of unbroken progress ahead of him, where everything will always be new and he'll keep obliviously brushing away all of the silly old fools who tell him how much he's grown.

One day it'll creep up on him. Years of his life will pass in a moment and he won't be able to understand where they've gone.

But it's ok. You can't hoard time. You just have to make the most of what you have.

Source B

This is an extract from a Victorian newspaper article of the 1800s. The writer explores how she feels now that her son has grown up.

Boy Lost

He had black eyes, with long lashes, red cheeks, and hair almost black and almost curly. He wore a crimson plaid jacket, with full trousers buttoned on, had a habit of whistling, and liked to ask questions. He was accompanied by a small black dog.

It is a long while now since he disappeared.

I have a very pleasant house and much company. My guests say, 'Ah, it is pleasant to be here! Everything has such an orderly, put-away look – nothing about under foot, no dirt!' But my eyes are aching for the sight of cut paper upon the floor; of tumbled-down card-houses; of wooden sheep and cattle; of pop-guns, bows and arrows, whips, tops and go-carts. I want to see crumbs on the carpet, and paste spilt on the kitchen table. I want to see the chairs and tables turned the wrong way about; yet these things used to fret me once.

They say, 'How quiet you are here; ah, one here may be at peace.' But my ears are aching for the pattering of little feet; for a hearty shout, a shrill whistle, for the crack of little whips, for the noise of drums and tin trumpets; yet these things made me nervous once.

They say – 'Ah, you are not tied at home. How delightful to be always at liberty for concerts, lectures, and parties! No responsibilities for you.' But I want responsibilities; I want to listen for the school bell of mornings; to give the last hasty wash and brush, and then to watch from the window nimble feet bounding away to school. I want to replace lost buttons and obliterate mud stains, fruit stains, treacle stains, and paints of all colours. I want to be sitting by a little crib of evenings, when weary little feet are at rest, and prattling voices are hushed, that mothers may sing their lullabies. They don't know their happiness then – those mothers. I didn't. All these things I called responsibilities once.

A manly figure stands before me now. He is taller than I, has thick black whiskers, and wears a frock coat, billowy shirt, and cravat. He has just come from college. He calls me mother, but I am rather unwilling to own him. He stoutly declares that he is my boy, and says he will prove it. He brings me his little boat to show the red stripe on the sail, and the name on the stern – 'Lucy Lowe' – our neighbour's little girl who, because of her long curls, and pretty round face, was the chosen favourite of my little boy. How the red comes to his face when he shows me the name on the boat!

And I see it all as plain as if it were written in a book. My little boy is lost, and my big boy will soon be. I wish he were still a little boy in a long white night gown, lying in his crib, with me sitting by, holding his hand in mine, pushing the curls back from his forehead, watching his eyelids droop, and listening to his deep breathing. If I only had my little boy again, how patient I would be! How much I would bear, and how little I would fret and scold! I can never have him back again; but there are still many mothers who haven't yet lost their little boys. I wonder if they know they are living their very best days; that now is the time to really enjoy their children!

I think if I had been more to my little boy I might now be more to my grown up one.

HOW TO ANSWER THE QUESTION

A few tips for how to work out exactly what the examiner wants here:

- Read the question carefully: it is only asking you about **the activities the boys enjoyed**.
- This is an eight mark question. However, don't be mislead into thinking you have to find four things from each article. What you have to do is take the evidence you find (maybe

2-3 things from each) and write them into a clear, intelligent summary. You'll get marks for evidence and marks for the quality of your linking/summarising.
- When you read through each article, underline anything which relates to the question. You should have underlined quotes like the following:
- **Source A:**
- *He loves running up to people and waiting for them to twang his lips like a ruler on a table.*
- *When he gets tired and barks gibberish in the middle of the room, he throws his entire body into it, like he's trying to shove the noise up a hill.*
- **Source B:**
- *the sight of cut paper upon the floor; of tumbled-down card-houses; of wooden sheep and cattle; of pop-guns, bows and arrows, whips, tops and go-carts.*
- *chairs and tables turned the wrong way about*
- *paints of all colours*
- Now, when you come to write up the answer, you should show that you're able to explain how the quotes give us an indication as to the character, and world, of each boy. Let's take a moment to look at how we do this successfully.

HOW TO ADD QUOTES INTO A SENTENCE

When you're explaining/analysing quotes, it is useful to know how to write them in such a way that each sentence flows smoothly one to the next. What you don't want to do is just drop a quote into a sentence so it stands out like a sore thumb.

So, aim to sneak those quotes in there so the whole thing is a joyful experience for Jeff and Jane (our friendly caffeine-fuelled examiners).

So, let's say we have the quote above: 'He loves running up to people and waiting for them to twang his lips'. We don't really want to use the whole quote, so how do we take a section of this and feed it into a sentence?

Perhaps something like this: 'In Source A, the boy "loves running up to people and waiting for them to twang his lips".' You see how the quote makes the sentence flow?

The above quote is quite a long one, but single words and short phrases are just as effective. For example, when talking about the second Source, you could say something like this: 'The mother misses "the noise of tin drums" and "paints of all colours".' This takes two quotes from different parts of the Source and pushes them together using the connective 'and'.

This is a good technique to use.

A SAMPLE GRADE 5-6 ANSWER

Here's the sample grade 5-6 answer from the answer paper. Remember: this isn't necessarily the whole answer, but rather it gives a good idea as to the sort of style the examiner will be looking for when awarding this grade range:

> In Source A the boy is only a year old but still makes his presence felt around the house by making lots of noise, especially when he's tired. He 'barks gibberish' in front of people, which suggests he is immature and likes the attention he gets from showing off. However, the boy in Source B is older and more independent and has real toys to play with, like 'drums and tin trumpets', which give him the opportunity to be more musical and more mature, rather than just shouting 'gibberish' in the middle of the room like the boy in Source A.

Let's take a moment to look at this in more depth:

- It uses quotes from both texts and feeds them nicely into the sentences
- It brings in a comparison between the two children by using the linking word 'However'

- It explains what these quotes tell us about the two children

It is a decent, solid, easy to read answer, but what it doesn't do is dig into smaller details, nor does it use particularly sophisticated language. Let's have a look now at a better answer - one that takes us up towards grade 7-8.

GOING HIGHER - GRADE 7 AND ABOVE

Here's the higher grade example:

> The activities of the boy in Source A are limited compared to the Victorian boy who has a wider choice of exciting and adventurous games to play. The toddler in Source A enjoys making a noise, exploring the sound effect of his own voice as he 'barks gibberish in the middle of the room.' His noisy outburst takes all his energy as 'he throws his entire body into it' showing how, at this self-centred stage of development, he just wants to express himself and attract attention. In contrast, the Victorian boy makes his own noise with 'a hearty shout' but has also been given purpose-built musical toys such as 'drums and tin trumpets'. He is at a different stage of maturity and needs more stimulation to develop his creativity, although perhaps both the boy's trumpet tooting and the toddler's 'gibberish' are just as irritating for any parent listening.

Can you see how it differs from the first example? This is what I can pick out:

- There are more quotes, and they are explained in a lot more detail. Look at how the writer uses particular phrases

to show the examiner they are analysing: 'showing how', 'he is at a different stage'.
- As in Paper 1, there is evidence of the student testing out theories: 'although perhaps'.
- Language is more advanced: 'self-centred stage of development', 'different stage of maturity', 'more stimulation'.
- Comparison is used well: one text referred to, then linked to the second by the linking phrase 'In contrast'. This enables the writer to say more about both - rather than trying to cram a comparison of both into every sentence, one Source is summarised in more depth before moving onto the other, showing the comparison when the writer moves from one Source to another.

YOUR TURN!

You're now going to try this for yourself. Rather than using two new Sources, let's use the same sources and have a different question:

> You need to refer to Source A and Source B for this question.
>
> The way each parent talks about their son tells us a lot about them.
>
> Use details from both sources to write a summary of the different ways the parents refer to their sons, and what this tells us about them as parents.
>
> [8 marks]

I've tried here to mirror the style of the other question as closely as possible, and you can be pretty sure that the question you have in the exam will have the same sort of structure.

Remember the structure:

- Make sure you understand what the question is asking you: underline the key points.

- Go through the passage and underline anything that can help you answer the question.
- Aim for between 3 and 4 quotes per Source - you might not use all of them.
- When writing them up, make sure you use the standard format:
- Introduce the quote;
- Bring the quote into the sentence so it flows smoothly;
- Explain how the quote answers the question.
- To link the two passages together, use a connecting phrase such as:
- *However,...*
- *In contrast,...*
- *The second Source contrasts the first by...*
- *Whereas Source A ...., Source B....*
- *Similarly,...*
- Try to conclude with a sentence that sums up the main difference between the two Sources.

Have a go with doing your own before reading mine below. Go on, try!

HERE'S MINE

Here's my higher grade response:

> In Source A, the writer describes the joys and stresses of being the father of a one year old boy. He humorously describes how he feels like the boy has 'always been part of the family', not because of any 'heart-eyed' reason, but because he hasn't 'slept for a year'. He emphasises his apparent confusion as a father by asking 'How is he one already?', consolidating this by stating that 'it's honestly quite hard to grasp' how quickly his son is growing up. However, he knows this is how things should be, and 'it's ok'. In contrast, Source B details the writer's wistful recollection of her son now that he has grown up. Interestingly, she initially refers to her son having grown up as him having 'disappeared', which suggests that

she no longer recognises the boy he once was - as if he is an entirely different person. She contrasts how others believe she should feel now that he has left home - 'how pleasant to be here… nothing about underfoot' - with how she really feels - 'my eyes are aching for a piece of cut paper upon the floor'. Whilst she recognises how to the outside world things seem calmer and more ordered than before, she wants 'responsibilities' and realises now that these were part of her happiness, even if she did not realise it before. Both Sources show how much love the writers have for their sons, but whilst the first is enjoying the process of seeing his son mature, the second longs to relive the times that she maybe did not fully appreciate whilst she was living them.

LOOKING AT THIS IN A BIT MORE DETAIL

I'd expect to give this near enough top marks. I hope you can see why:

- It uses a lot of quotes and always explains what we learn about the writer's view of being a parent;
- It uses a lot of sophisticated language: 'consolidating', 'wistful recollection', 'Whilst she recognises….'
- It uses some advanced ways of quoting, by using dashes (parentheses) to separate the quotes from the sentence (we saw this in Paper 1);
- It sums the two Sources up in the final sentence, saying one more clever thing;
- It digs under the surface of the Source, looking both at what it said on the surface, and what is implicit/implied. In other words, the more obvious stuff and the more subtle stuff. This is what you have to do to get the top marks.

QUESTION 3

This question asks you to analyse a short section of one of the Sources very closely. The Assessment Objective asks you to look at **words, phrases, language features, language techniques and sentence forms,** and **use evidence to back up your ideas**. So it's a bit like questions 2 and 3 together from Paper 1. And, funnily enough, it's worth the same number of marks as Paper 1 questions 2 and 3 put together: 12 marks.

Here's the question from the 2017 paper:

> You now need to refer only to Source A from lines 18 to 28.
>
> How does the writer use language to describe his son?

Whilst the question itself is quite simple, what it is asking you to is potentially challenging, as this is the first time in the Language exam that you're being asked to closely analyse a short passage.

A WORD ON ANALYSIS

You'll no doubt heard your teacher talk about the importance of analysis when getting the higher marks, but might have been unsure as to what they mean. You'll also have seen that I refer to analysis and explanation together in this guide.

There's a good reason for that.

They're pretty much one and the same thing.

Obviously, the word 'explain' has other meanings (such as 'young man, please explain why you ate all the pies'), but when we refer to explanation in English, what we mean is this:

Explain how the quote answers the question.

Your teachers may have talked a lot about PEE - Point, Evidence, Explanation - and that's fine. I prefer PEAL:

- Point - you open the sentence by introducing what you're going to talk about
- Evidence - you bring in the quote or direct reference to the text
- Analysis - you explain how the quote answers the question
- Link - you then link to the next point

That's really it. What an analytical approach does is force you into finding quotes, as it's hard to analyse unless you have some evidence to talk about. This might be a short quote, series of quotes, or direct reference to a structural element of the text.

With that in mind, let's look at how we go about planning for analysis.

THE PASSAGE

I've pulled out the relevant section from the Source below:

> A year ago, he was a sleepy ball of scrunched-up flesh, but is now determinedly his own person. I can see everyone in him – me, my wife, my parents – yet he's already separate from all of us. He's giddy and silly. He's a show-off, albeit one who's irrationally terrified of my dad. He loves running up to people and waiting for

them to twang his lips like a ruler on a table. When he gets tired and barks gibberish in the middle of the room, he throws his entire body into it, like he's trying to shove the noise up a hill.

With every tiny development – every new step he takes, every new tooth and sound and reaction that comes along to ambush us – we're confronted with a slightly different child.

Photos of him taken in the summer seem like dispatches from a million years ago. Photos of him taken last week seem like a different boy. He's blasting ahead as far as he can. He's leaving milestone after milestone in his wake and tiny parts of me along with them.

I know what you're thinking, and you'd be right: that's not much text to write a 12 mark answer from!

But, we're now moving into territory where we can really excel: because it's those students (aka you) **who really get into small details** and 'say a lot about a little rather than a little about a lot' (remember that one as we'll come back to it) that will do particularly well here.

For those of you who've done poetry analysis before (and I'm guessing it's most of you out there), a good way to go about this is to **approach this question like poetry analysis**.

The only thing you won't focus on is line length and line breaks - but pretty much everything else can be analysed:

- Language techniques, such as alliteration, simile, metaphor, repetition etc.
- Parts of speech - adjective, pronoun etc.
- Sentence length
- Punctuation

WHAT'S JEFF LOOKING FOR HERE?

Our friendly examiner Jeff will be looking for is 'how writers use language and structure to achieve effects and influence readers, using relevant subject terminology to support their views'.

Providing you look at both language and structure, find quotes and use the right language when analysing them, you can't go far wrong.

And how long is long enough? For a 12 mark answer I'd suggest a couple of paragraphs. So probably about 1/2 to 3/4 of a page in your answer paper.

If you have big writing you might stretch to a page. Any more than that and you'll be robbing time for the last question.

And you don't want to do that, now do you?

HOW TO PREPARE FOR ANALYSIS

This is the same as Paper 1: you underline relevant words and phrases, jot some notes down in the margin, and use the standard structure we've talked about a lot (PEAL or PEE or whatever works for you).

With the above Source, you have underlined quotes like these and added a few notes:

- 'sleepy ball of scrunched up flesh' - neither ball nor flesh sound particularly human - as if he wasn't yet a person
- Use of parentheses ' - me, my wife, my parents -' separates the boy from his family - backed up by following quote
- Short sentence that follows - assonance - both words almost onomatopoeic - 'giddy and silly' - sound of words links to boy's actions
- 'Like a ruler on the table' - childlike simile emphasising boy's silliness
- 'Like he's trying to shove the noise up the hill' - lovely simile - stressing how much effort boy puts into life

..and so on.

You'll find that, the more you do this, the easier it gets. You're looking for anything which stands out, paints a picture in your mind, anything that's vivid or unusual.

Remember it's how the words are written on the page as well as the words themselves - so long and short sentences, use of parentheses (dashes or brackets), commas and so on.

This is **'saying a lot about a little'** - taking one small detail and teasing as much information as possible out of it.

Let's look at how the mark scheme deals with two different answers to this, before we go on to have a go ourselves. You might want to try answering the above question before moving on to the two sample answers. It's up to you!

THE GRADE 5-6 ANSWER

Here's the mark schemes sample. Again, it's not the whole answer, just part of the answer. It give us an idea of what this grade will look like:

> The writer starts with a metaphor to describe his new born baby son as 'a sleepy ball of scrunched-up flesh'. The image of a 'sleepy ball' gives a sense of the baby curled up, cosy and snuggled, whilst the phrase 'scrunched-up flesh' shows how difficult it was to make out his son's features. The word 'scrunched' suggests that the baby's face is crumpled and creased.

As you can see, it's clearly written, uses quotes well, and with some explanation. So why doesn't it get the top marks?

By now you probably know what I'm about to say, and if that's the case then well done you! You're well on the way to a grade 9 in your GCSE in 'getting inside the examiner's head'.

Here's why:

- Whilst it does use language clearly, there's no real sophistication in the word choice. It's pretty basic.
- There is no use of any technical language - 'image', 'phrase', 'word'.
- There is some analysis but it is basic: 'gives a sense of', ''shows how'.
- There is no reference to anything to do with sentence forms or langauge techniques - it only focuses on the words themselves.

Now you might ask how the examiner can mark your paper given such a short passage to work from, but remember - Jeff and Jane are experienced at this. They know what they're looking for and will know when an answer ticks enough boxes to get the higher grades.

And now you know too! The above is pretty good, but I think we can do better, don't you?

GOING HIGHER - GRADES 7 AND ABOVE

So, the higher grade sample looks like this:

> The writer uses metaphorical language to describe his son as 'a sleepy ball', providing the reader with an endearing image of a contented infant curled up, still in the foetal position, suggesting he is very newly born. The adjective 'sleepy' conjures up the image of the peace and tranquillity associated with a drowsy baby and a sense of innocence. The phrase 'scrunched-up flesh' sounds affectionate but comical, and implies that the child's individual features are unformed and unrecognisable – he looks just like any other baby.

You can probably see straight away how this differs - how this is both 'detailed and perceptive' (to use the language from the mark scheme).

Here are the main ingredients:

- Straight away it uses technical language: 'metaphorical'
- It refers to 'the reader' - remember, this is all about the

effect of language and structure on the reader, so why not refer directly to them? This is a good way to introduce analysis.
- More sophisticated word choice: 'endearing', 'foetal'. There really isn't a way for me to teach this level of language I'm afraid - the only way to learn is to read lots and to use a thesaurus to build your word power. It's why I always say that kids who read lots of fiction are often much better writers, because they've built up a bigger vocabulary. But don't worry - it's never too late to start…
- A variety of what I have referred to before as 'analytical signposts' - phrases which show the examiner that analysis will follow: 'providing the reader', 'conjures up an image', 'implies that'.
- Evidence of digging deeper - the 'scrunched up flesh' is 'affectionate but comical', and the dash at the end of the last sentence shows the student adding one more thing. That's what it's all about - just adding one more thing when you analyse.

We can now have a think about how we might answer a similar question on Source B.

YOUR TURN!

Let's use a similar question, but choose part of Source B instead.

> You now need to refer only to Source B from lines 5 to 13
>
> How does the writer use language to describe her son's effect on her life when he was young?

Here's the passage:

> I have a very pleasant house and much company. My guests say, 'Ah, it is pleasant to be here! Everything has such an orderly, put-away look – nothing about under foot, no dirt!' But my eyes are aching for the sight of cut paper upon the floor; of tumbled-down card-houses; of wooden sheep and cattle; of pop-guns, bows and arrows, whips, tops and go-carts. I want to see crumbs on the carpet, and paste spilt on the kitchen table. I want to see the chairs and tables turned the wrong way about; yet these things used to fret me once.
>
> They say, 'How quiet you are here; ah, one here may be at peace.' But my ears are aching for the pattering of little feet; for a hearty

shout, a shrill whistle, for the crack of little whips, for the noise of drums and tin trumpets; yet these things made me nervous once.

Go through the usual drill: underline any quotes which tell us something about the boy's impact on her life.

- Look at both the words used and how they're broken up using punctuation.
- Look at the sounds of words as well as the words themselves
- Look at repetition
- Look at the repeated semi colon (;) at the end of each paragraph and its effect

Underline and make notes. Think about how you'll structure the answer, remembering that the best way to do this is to begin at the beginning and work your way through the passage.

HERE'S MY SAMPLE

This is the opening to mine. You'll see it's quite similar in structure to the sample 7-8 answer we've just looked at:

> The writer begins by emphasising how pleasant her life apparently now is. The first sentence sets the scene, the adjective 'very' drawing attention to how happy she should now be. This is emphasised by her reference to what her guests tell her: by referring to her home as being 'orderly' and having 'no dirt', the writer suggests that her guests believe she is lucky to finally have the house to herself. Even the use of the exclamation mark draws attention to them being happy for her, and perhaps surprised at how tidy her house now is. However, the following list of things she misses indicates to the reader that all is not as positive as it seems. She begins this list by saying that her 'eyes are aching', emphasising just how much she wants her little boy back. The repetition that follows ('of…of…of') builds a picture of a home which used to have its surfaces covered in the sorts of toys and

games small children love: there is a sense of things accumulating, of a messy home but one filled with energy and love.

…and so on….

CAN YOU SEE WHAT I DID?

I'm sure you can. Just look at the first two sentences.

- The first makes the initial **point** (how pleasant her life apparently is).
- The second brings in the **quote**, saying how it **answers** that initial point. It also brings in a part of speech - the 'adjective'.
- The beginning of the third **links** these points together - 'This is emphasised by…'.

Again - just about practice. No more, no less.

Have a go at writing the entire answer, following the same structure above.

QUESTION 4

They certainly save the best till last. Or the worst. Depends on whether you like a challenge.

Here's the final question, worth 16 marks. Only four marks more than the last question. But you seem to have to do so much more!

> For this question, you need to refer to the whole of Source A, together with the whole of Source B.
>
> Compare how the writers convey their different perspectives and feelings about their children growing up.
>
> In your answer, you could:
>
> compare their different perspectives and feelings
>
> compare the methods the writers use to convey their different perspectives and feelings
>
> support your response with references to both texts.
>
> [16 marks]

Remember those suggested bullet points from Paper 1? The same applies here: which is why I'll politely shout them to you again:

YOU SHOULD ABSOLUTELY DEFINITELY REFER TO THESE BULLET POINTS IN YOUR ANSWER. IGNORE 'COULD': IT'S CRAZY NOT TO USE EXACTLY THE THINGS THE EXAMINER WILL BE LOOKING FOR.

OK, shout over. I'm out of breath now.

The main difference between this question and every other question (save for question 2, which touches on this) is that this question is all about **comparison**. How both texts explore the same subject in different ways.

In this case, it's all about the **writers' perspectives and feelings on their children growing up**. Not what the kids do, or what they did, but how the writers feel about their kids getting older.

It's so important with this question that you take the time to fully understand what the question is asking. As you could easily spend the whole answer talking about the children, rather than their parents' attitudes towards the ageing process. And that would be wrong!

I can guarantee you loads of students will do this. Aren't you glad you won't be one of them?

SO WHAT'S JEFF LOOKING FOR HERE?

I'm glad you asked me that - you're learning. It's quite simple: the assessment objectives say that Jeff has to assess you on how well you **compare writers' ideas and perspectives, as well as how these are conveyed, across the two texts**. No more, no less.

However, I think this is one of the hardest things to do, and whilst it has its uses out there in the real world, they're pretty limited. Still, like writing a story about a bus journey, this is what you're being asked to do, so this is what you have to do. Deal with it, as the sports coach might say.

This is how I suggest you go about preparing for this answer:

- As always - go through each source, underlining anything that refers to the writers' attitudes towards their children getting older. You're looking for how they comment on the things their children do and say, and how these are changing (or in the case of Source B, how they have changed). Ultimately it's about how quickly time passes and how important it is to enjoy things as they happen.
- Now, look for the similar themes and ideas that emerge from this exercise: for example, how the writers physically describe their child getting older, or the child's impact on his environment and the people around him. You should aim to find 3-4 points of comparison - so between 6 and quotes.
- You're now going to begin by introducing one point, in the same way you've done time and again (you're getting quite expert at this by now, aren't you). You'll bring in a quote from Source A, then talk about how this quote answers the question.
- From here, you move on to Source B, bringing in a quote and explaining how this differs from Source A.
- For the higher marks you'll then make a concluding remark about these differences, before moving on to the next point.
- At the end, you'll want a concluding statement, which summarises, in no more than one or two sentences, the key similarities or differences between the two texts and how they treat the subject matter.

Let's see this in action with our two differently graded answers.

THE GRADE 5-6 ANSWER

We start (as always) with our solid grade 5-6 sample from the mark scheme. And, as always, this isn't necessarily the whole answer. You'd probably look to write another paragraph of this length:

> The writer of Source A, a modern father, is both saddened and pleased by his son's growth. He finds it difficult to accept that time is moving so quickly; he 'blinked' and his son is already a year old. However, the pleasure he feels is also obvious, using phrases like 'blasting ahead' to suggest his son is metaphorically taking off like a rocket before his eyes. In contrast, the writer of Source B, who presents a Victorian mother's perspective, has a negative reaction to her son growing into a young man. She conveys a sense of loss at his independence, even using the phrase 'My little boy is lost'. By using the word 'lost' we understand that she no longer sees herself as part of his life and she regrets that he is no longer dependent on her to 'replace lost buttons'.

Here are its strengths:

- It compares the two writers' perspectives on their children clearly;

- It makes reference to the methods the writers use - 'metaphorically', 'conveys a sense of loss';
- It uses quotes well;
- It shows that the student understands the different periods the writers are writing from - 'a modern father', 'Victorian mother's perspective'.

As in the other examples, it lacks more sophisticated language, and doesn't go into much depth when focusing in on language techniques. Let's look at the higher grade answer and we can see the differences quite clearly.

AIMING HIGHER - GRADE 7 AND ABOVE

Here's the higher grade answer:

> Heritage, a 21st Century father, is incredulous at how the first year has flown; he 'blinked' and the transformation from baby to toddler seemed to happen overnight. There is clearly a tone of fatherly pride as he describes his son's growing independence; 'blasting ahead' suggests he is powering through each stage of development with unstoppable force. The Victorian mother of Source B, however, although perhaps secretly proud of his 'manly figure,' conveys her feelings of sadness that her son no longer needs her: 'It is a long while now since he disappeared,' implying the loss is literal, whereas it is in fact metaphorical - the mother has emotionally, not physically, lost him. She uses a repetitive structure to emphasise her tone of regret. Each paragraph begins with the guests' views on the positive aspects of life without young children, which is, ironically, the opposite of how the mother feels.

I think you can see straight away that this is more sophisticated and goes deeper into both texts:

- Word choice is more advanced: 'incredulous', 'growing independence', 'tone of regret';
- It analyses the writers' methods well, using our analytical signposts - 'suggest he is…', 'conveys her feelings…', 'implying the loss…';
- It hones in on details - 'uses a repetitive structure', 'Each paragraph begins with the guests' views…'
- The student shows they understand irony - which in itself is quite sophisticated. In a nutshell, irony is a technique writers use contrast the surface appearance of something with its underlying truth. In this case, the positive surface opinion of the guests with how the mother really feels.

We can now apply this to another question on the same two texts.

YOUR TURN!

Let's have a think about another question along the same lines:

> For this question, you need to refer to the whole of Source A, together with the whole of Source B.
>
> Compare how the writers convey their different perspectives and feelings about being a parent.
>
> In your answer, you could:
>
> compare their different perspectives and feelings
>
> compare the methods the writers use to convey their different perspectives and feelings
>
> support your response with references to both texts.
>
> [16 marks]

Rather than focusing only on the children growing up, this question asks you to look carefully at the writers' views of themselves as parents - their roles, responsibilities, successes and failures.

HERE'S MY SAMPLE ANSWER

I will assume you've been through the usual planning process here: don't cut corners with this and try to plough straight into writing as this is a recipe for confusion.

Here's one paragraph that takes the same approach as all the other grade 7-8 answers we've looked at:

> As a 21st Century writer, Heritage seems to feel both a sense of great joy and at times confusion in his role as a father. The opening paragraph, in which he refers to the year since his son's birth as being the 'longest and shortest', emphasises this sense of confusion: he adds to this by saying that, whilst it feels like his son 'has always been part of' his family, this is not in any 'obnoxious' way, but rather because he hasn't 'slept for a year'. Heritage shows here the truth of parenting, at just how rewarding but also how challenging it is.
>
> The writer in Source B, on the other hand, longs for the challenges of the past, and misses her son and his impact on her life greatly. Her lovingly detailed description of her son in the first paragraph, with his 'long lashes' and 'red cheeks', conjure up an image of a healthy, vibrant child, one that left a considerable mark on her life. By referring to his maturing as having 'disappeared', however, she brings a note of sadness into her description, as if the boy she once knew no longer exists. It is as if the act of parenting this boy defined her, and she no longer knows who she is now that he has grown up.

Have a go at continuing this on in the same way, making another point about source A before moving onto source B.

PAPER 2 SECTION B

INTRODUCTION

Phew! That was quite an epic section, wasn't it? Seemed a lot more involved than Paper 1. But this makes sense - the whole point of these exams is that they get progressively harder.

Those that succeed are those who stick it out to the end and raise their game when the going gets tough. And other sports-related metaphors.

We come onto the last section of your Language exam. Once you put your pen down on this you need never do another Language lesson again. Unless you choose it at A-Level. And not many people do as Literature is more popular.

Or you have to retake. Which won't happen with you after you've read this guide, now will it?

(Disclaimer - I can't take any responsibility for how well you do in your exam. All I can do is share my wisdom and cross my fingers come exam time. But you knew that!)

Let's have a look at what Section B is asking you to do.

SECTION B SUMMARY

This section marks you on three main things:

- How well you communicate with your writing, using the right style for the purpose and audience;
- How well you organise your ideas, using the right structure to make it clear;
- Your word choice, sentence structure, spelling and punctuation.

Up to 24 marks for the first two bullet points, and another 16 marks for the third bullet point.

You'll only get one question, so if you don't like it, you'll have to make the best of it!

THE DIFFERENT TYPES OF WRITING THAT MIGHT COME UP IN THE EXAM

Now, I'm not going to go into loads of detail about the different types of non-fiction writing that might crop up. Hopefully by now you'll have spent time in class writing to inform, explain, argue or persuade.

My guess (and I have been known to be wrong) is that they'll generally ask you to write either to persuade, or to argue. Argument writing (sometimes referred to as discursive writing) is in many ways the easiest to teach, as it follows a set pattern. We'll look at this when we turn to the exam paper question in a moment

THE QUESTION

Here's the Section B question:

> 'Parents today are over-protective. They should let their children take part in adventurous, even risky, activities to prepare them for later life.'
>
> Write an article for a broadsheet newspaper in which you argue for or against this statement.
>
> (24 marks for content and organisation and
>
> 16 marks for technical accuracy)

HOW TO APPROACH THIS QUESTION

There are two things you need to take from this question:

- **What** it is asking you to do (the subject and writing style);
- **Who** it is asking you to do it for (the audience).

In this case, you're being asked to write a piece of argument for a broadsheet newspaper.

Yes, I know what you're thinking. No. One. Reads. Broadsheets. Any. More. Apart from examiners perhaps. Everyone reads news on their phone or iPad. Maybe one day Jeff will join the real world.

But for now, you only need to know one thing: broadsheets like The Telegraph are more intellectual and formal than tabloids like The Sun and Daily Mail. What's even more ironic is that most of the broadsheets (so called because they have big pages) are now tabloid in size!

So if you're asked to write for a broadsheet audience, use more formal language, and if it's a tabloid you can be more conversational. That will tick the 'writing for a particular audience' box.

PLANNING THE ANSWER

Notice that the question says 'argue for or against'? Well, this doesn't mean that you only present one side of the argument. Oh no. You should make sure you show the other point of view as well, so that you can argue against it.

Here's how I'd approach planning the answer:

- On your answer paper, divide your page into two columns.
- At the top of the first column write 'For', and at the top of the second 'Against'.
- Under the 'For' column write down as many reasons as you can think that agree with the statement that kids should take part in risky activities. It doesn't matter whether you personally agree or not - try to remain neutral and think about what any advantages might be.
- Under the 'Against' column, guess what? That's right: you list all the reasons why exposing children to risky activities is not such a good idea, and how children should be protected. Again, they don't have to be your own opinions, just what some people might think.

WRITING THE ANSWER

- Now, when you write your answer, you begin by introducing the subject. As it's an opinion piece (not hard news but rather someone's point of view on a subject) you could begin by referring to a fictional news story which got you thinking about this topic. In this case, maybe it's a story about a child who was killed or injured whilst taking part in a risky activity. This will make your article sound more 'newsy'.
- What you should then do is state your point of view, quite clearly.
- At the start of the next paragraph, state one reason for why you agree or disagree with the statement. Then bring in some evidence to back this up.
- A good technique is to then bring in another point of view, one that disagrees with you and gives an alternative perspective (something from the opposite column in your notes). You can then show how wrong they are, and why.
- Bring in some facts and statistics to make your arguments sound more credible. Don't worry: these can be made up (just don't make them too unrealistic).
- You continue in this way until the end, where you sum up why your point of view is the right one.

SEEING THIS IN ACTION

It's easier to see this in action. Here's the opening of my response to this question. Note the headline and subheading, to make it seem more 'newspapery':

> **When risk means reward: the importance of adventure in kids' lives**
>
> *E.Head argues that risk is as much a part of learning as anything taught at school.*

The news yesterday of the two teenage boys seriously injured whilst attempting to climb The Shard brought home with clarity how much kids enjoy taking risks. There is an argument to say that we should make sure we keep our children close, that it's our responsibility to make sure nothing bad happens to them. After all, if the two boys been properly looked after, would this have happened to them?

But I don't think it's as simple as that. I believe that risk is a fundamental part of growing up, and that without it we risk something far greater: our children turning into adults with no imagination and no lust for life. And that may well be worse than the bumps and bruises they get along the way.

One of the main reasons why children need to take risks is that they need to understand the limits of their bodies. I can well remember trying to climb trees that were way beyond me, and suffering as a result. Yes, it may be safer in the short term to stay indoors, but if all children do is sit at home and play video games, they will not only never learn about their physical capabilities, but will more than likely put on a lot of weight. In a recent study, more than 60% of children below the age of 12 are now classed as obese: that's a terrifying statistic and demonstrates how important it is for kids to get out there and enjoy the world.

Another important reason for taking risks in life is that, as we get older, we will be confronted with them without having any choice. It's easy being a kid in many ways: all our big choices are made for us. But as we grow into adults, we will naturally have to make tough choices - and it is those adults who took risks when they were younger who are more likely to be successful when older, as they are willing to take the plunge when need be…

Hopefully you can see all the bullet points above ticked. A newsy opening, my point of view, a counter argument and me disagreeing, a made up percentage statistic, and so on. Each argument is on a new paragraph: this keeps the paragraphs nice and short and makes it easier to read.

A FEW USEFUL LINKING PHRASES

- When writing argument, there are a few phrases that are useful to learn.
- 'On the one hand… On the other hand…'
- 'Some might say that… However, I believe that…'
- 'There is an argument to say that…'
- 'Furthermore,…' - to extend your argument
- 'Moreover,…' - same
- 'Conversely,…' - to bring in a counter argument - another point of view

YOUR TURN!

Here are three questions to get you practising writing argument-based responses:

1. 'Teaching through gaming is a valuable way to get children interested in school. Video games can have enormous potential to both motivate and teach important concepts in a number of subjects.'

Write an article for a broadsheet newspaper in which you argue for or against this statement.

2. 'Children today have too much freedom. There is simply not enough discipline in families nowadays, which means children are growing up without boundaries.'

Write an article for a tabloid newspaper in which you argue for or against this statement.

3. 'The major problems in the world come through money. Without money we would have a much more peaceful society.'

Write an article for a teen's magazine in which you argue for or against this statement.

Remember to go through the same planning stage, and use the linking words and phrases where appropriate.

NOW IT'S TIME TO SAY GOODBYE

You see: that wasn't so bad, was it. You got to the end! Well done.

If this book has changed your life in some small way, I'd be grateful if you could leave a review. Here's the page to do so - thank you!

Do also check out my other books in the same series:

- Macbeth for GCSE Literature
- An Inspector Calls for GCSE Literature
- Essay Peasy! How to write any GCSE essay with ease.

Best of luck and remember: examiners are human too…

Printed in Great Britain
by Amazon